Inside Writing:
A Reader's Notebook

INSIDE WRITING:
A READER'S
NOTEBOOK

MARTHE ROBERT

HARVESTER PRESS . SUSSEX

HUMANITIES PRESS . NEW JERSEY

This edition first published in Great Britain in 1981 by
THE HARVESTER PRESS LIMITED
Publisher: John Spiers
16 Ship Street, Brighton, Sussex

and in the USA by
HUMANITIES PRESS INC.
Atlantic Highlands, New Jersey 07716

Translated by
SACHA RABINOVITCH

First published in France as
Livre de lectures
Editions Bernard Grasset, Paris, 1977

British Library Cataloguing in Publication Data

Robert, Marthe
  Inside writing.
  1. Literature
  I. Title
  800   PN45.R57

  ISBN 0-85527-737-8

  Humanities Press Inc.
    ISBN 0-391-02274-1

Photoset in ¹²/₁₅pt Bembo by
Photobooks (Bristol) Limited
28 Midland Road, St Philips, Bristol
and printed in Great Britain by
Redwood Burn Limited, Trowbridge and Esher

Since I can't stop thinking about literature and especially about the relation between writing and living, I've decided to jot down here in a sort of undated diary the thoughts and queries which occur to me in connection with what I'm reading, regardless of the genre or even the quality of the text. I have no intention of quoting works or authors in order to criticise them—even in the scientific and technical sense this word has acquired—but rather to note how indefinable, ungraspable and obscure literature can be under the reassuring aspect of a classified phenomenon. I want to find out from the books that come my way what's happening to literature as a whole, what accounts for its remarkable social influence and from what mysterious source its enduring fascination derives.

*

Of reading as a theoretical and practical form of

suicide.—The German poet August von Platen knew what he was talking about when he wrote to a friend: *Ich habe mein Leben verlesen*, which means 'I've spent my life reading', or, to take the original short cut which can, anyhow, only be followed circuitously: 'My whole life has passed away in reading, instead of living I read and books have turned me into a living corpse.' Though the author of these commonplace and terrifying words didn't literally exchange his life for the printed page, for Don Quixote—who shared the same misguided passion for books and, probably, the same reasons for indulging it—it was obviously his master. For the quixotic reader tragically (or comically) confuses life and literature, not only to satisfy a legitimate intellectual need, but mainly to compensate for an innate inadequacy in his spiritual make-up, a kind of deficiency of being that isolates him in a limbo mid-way between dream and reality. Naturally ill-equipped for the responsibilities and hardships of this world, he seeks in books the absolute elsewhere in which, free from the necessity of being a man among men, he will be able to believe he has recovered from his ridiculous infirmity. And indeed he does find in an infinite number of printed characters that elsewhere from which he expects salvation, since with the help of literature his life has become little more than a protracted suicide. Thus the confirmed reader, the one who reads himself to death, does more than betray the utmost intellectual depravity, he exposes the duplicity of an art that, under cover of portraying life actually promotes death.

*

'The comic tyranny of the printed word.' (J. Vallès): few question it though it oppresses many. Yet in fact it ought to be submitted to a truly radical criticism, deeply sceptical of the over-obvious, the over-simple and the over-familiar which is always taken for granted.

*

'The very gift of style, of form and expression, is nothing else than this cool and fastidious attitude towards humanity; you might say there has to be this impoverishment and devastation as a preliminary condition.' (*Tonio Kröger*). Thomas Mann spoke from experience, but his self-criticism is a model for all criticism, if indeed the two can ever be strictly independent.

*

E. M. Cioran: 'On the inconvenience of being born.' The honesty of his first person singular in an age when every writer assumes the right to speak for all! Cioran's 'I' is so much truer and more respectable than the 'he' or the 'we' which is made to speak for all mankind by anybody who is able to put pen to paper. His 'I shall never get used to living' is irrefutable. What a pity, though, that he gets involved in metaphysics. It makes the book seem less genuine.

*

People who are preoccupied with spiritual matters can't help hating the idea of having been born. But those who have any insight know that what irks them in the inevitability of birth is the fact that they are 'limited' by the parents who bore them. To be born is less intolerable than to be pre-determined once and for all by a vast accumulation of past events, the already there, the already done, the already said and thought. And it is with this compact mass, where barely differentiated biological and sociological factors reinforce each other, that the novelist and the poet have to contend. For a writer, whatever he may consciously wish to communicate, can only express his refusal to be one more link in the chain of generations. To such rebels a successful literary career often makes suicide seem a good deal less inevitable—though it cannot always prevent it.

*

The deterioration of language seems to be a chronic historical disease bemoaned by every generation in turn. The current epidemic conforms largely to the general syndrome. What makes it different is that it occurs at a time when linguistic problems are grossly overrated, so that the process is in fact accelerated by that which should logically have slowed it down if not actually stopped it altogether.

*

Jargon always presupposes an ideology which wants, for some reason or other, to avoid being too easily understood. Thus the purification or liberation of thought necessarily involves a critical rejection of any jargon written or spoken. And what is generally dismissed as a *quibble on words* is not the pastime of shallow minds but the one quarrel worth picking.

*

Our attitude to so-called inspired poets, artists or novelists. Once they have been acknowledged and granted a solid posthumous reputation we automatically take their side against the bourgeois, the philistine or the nobody unlucky enough to have opposed them during their lives. In the eyes of posterity or even sometimes of contemporaries, parents, wives, friends, mistresses, landlords and creditors are always in the wrong when they try to hold their own against a genius rather than consent to be betrayed, sacrificed or rejected by him. And this, not on account of his singular virtues, but because of the high regard we have for his mission. We do not object to Dostoevsky's gambling away night after night all the money he owed to his landlord—indeed what could be more natural since gambling is part of his image? But all his biographers are unanimous (for once) in condemning the landlord who, after waiting patiently for months, finally takes the case to court. Posterity won't allow the poor German landlord to plead his rights, his honesty or his ignorance of Russian literature—indeed most likely of any literature. He was in the wrong since he transgressed an implicit law of our cultural code, according to which a tenant of genius, even when he has not yet proved himself such, is entitled to free board and lodging.

*

Thus notwithstanding our advanced ideas we still believe in the mythological favourite of the gods. We are even persuaded that the common herd instinctively recognises his innate superiority, can't help but venerate him, and is willing furthermore to exempt him from active service in the struggle for life (never mind if none of this is confirmed by experience: those who feel differently are condemned forthwith). True this remarkable law of exemption doesn't seem to give much satisfaction to its beneficiaries who tend to see themselves as very far from privileged beings whom nobody understands and appreciates—if not as downright unlucky. At least this is the attitude they usually adopt when writing about the traditional conflict between the artist and society—which is only an exaggerated form of that between the individual and the world on which all great literature is based. Strange though, that among the writers most given to reflections on their trade, no one as far as I know has felt personally challenged by all those put-upon landlords and thus compelled to reconsider the mysterious case of the artist who, for some inexplicable reason, is entitled to ignore the rights of his fellow mortals. The novelists portrayed in their own books never raise the question (even Gide who detects something of the money-forging writer in himself, is very far from confessing to sponging). At most they observe with Thomas Mann 'the impoverishment and devastation' of those involved in their trade, without wondering, however, how such an infirmity can further their cause as masters and guides. On the other hand, notwithstanding their need for accuracy and

justice, they never show any surprise at the preferential treatment which exempts them from walking in
step with other men and allows them to stand still in
the middle of existence to blacken a white page in
order that they may reveal all those things life can't
possibly know about itself. No, they are not surprised
to be practically kept by society in exchange for
services which, though highly valued, have no easily
identifiable use. And such a lack of surprise is so much
part of our way of thinking that no one would dream
of even noticing it.

*

Funnily enough Kafka is the only writer to have
discussed the conspiracy of silence surrounding art's
prerogatives, and the source of its powerful attraction.
He who was wholly dedicated to his art ('I am and
desire to be nothing but literature . . . '. 'Everything
that isn't literature bores me and I hate it . . .') and
ultimately sacrificed his life to this ruthless idol,
invariably represents the artist as quite unremarkable
apart from his stubborn pursuit of a meaningless goal
and from his feebleness, irresponsibility and redund-
ancy. In their various disguises these insignificant yet
unusual beings are all equally adept at gratuitous self-
torture whose motives they refuse to discuss. They
cannot be deterred from their obsessions, and shut

themselves away in a mock paradise where they lead miserable, parasitic, puerile lives. They are hopelessly doomed from the start but when retribution strikes it is hard to tell if they are condemned as fanatics or as martyrs, as dreamers or as charlatans. Kafka's satire on the idolisation of art is the most cruel ever to have been written and should, if properly understood, discredit all the ridiculous ideas which one generation of readers after another has imputed to him. (It is not properly understood for two reasons: first because of all the taboos on the subject, and secondly because everyone is so busy trying to find out what Kafka *meant* but *didn't say* that nobody can see the words he wrote).

Kafka's artists are notable mainly for their inability to come to terms with life and to assume responsibilities. Thus the Hunger Artist who can't or won't earn his daily bread turns his aptitude for starvation into an art. In this way art and the inevitable death it involves merge into a single image—the only thing that distinguishes him from the common starveling is that his artistic creation *is* his hunger, hunger become flesh and objective. Such artists create in a vacuum unaware of the crowds flocking to their exhibitions and totally uninterested in public censure or acclaim. Why then this self-imposed torture which neither human nor divine law requires from them? Why do they choose to live a life so unnatural that it amounts to a slow and painful suicide? In the pursuit of what ideal or in the hope of what salvation do they spend their time on a flying trapeze or exhibited behind the bars of a fairground cage? Why won't they talk about their strange occupation? That is what the Dog, who in one of Kafka's stories tries to penetrate the barrier of silence society maintains on the subject, would like to know. Not a member of the artist class himself, but one of those rational, inquisitive, 'cynical' intellectuals of whom Joseph K. and K. the Land Surveyor are the best known representatives, the Dog is nonetheless entitled by his ambiguous feelings of attraction and repulsion, terror and veneration for art, to talk about it, if not from the inside—the inside is precisely what eludes him—at least as an enthusiastic witness and observer. His childhood encounter with seven dog-musicians emerging unexpectedly from the dark was a major event, a bewildering revelation which altered the course of his life. These performers from whom music emanated as though by magic introduced him at an early age to a nocturnal world of terrifying beauty where creatures both marvellous and obscene openly defy the most sacred canine laws without any apparent fear of retribution. The inexperienced pup can't believe his eyes! No sooner recovered from the shock he runs off to question all and sundry on his extraordinary experience which, after all, may well have been a dream. Thus begin his investigations on art, soon to be complemented by an active enquiry into the origins of food and the problem of hunger—as if these two kinds of mystery were so intimately related that they must either elucidate one another or both remain equally impenetrable. But naturally enough the Dog achieves absolutely nothing. All the questions he puts to his fellow dogs are met with silence—an indulgent, half-amused silence at first which gradually becomes disapproving as the Dog approaches maturity and still persists in trying to force an issue.

The dogs resist every method of interrogation, but they can't stop the questions from flowing. Indeed their silence stimulates curiosity, not only in what they are concealing but also in their motives for conceal-ment. Thus in the incident about the aerial dogs—one of the most ruthlessly comic attacks on art ever written—the hero is faced with two sets of questions each cancelling out the other: 'Why do such dogs float in the air?' and 'Why can't one get a single word of explanation from them?' Since everybody ignores, or pretends to ignore the phenomenon's objective cause and since the aerial dogs refuse to reveal it, the question probing the extent of knowledge is excluded from knowledge by the question concerning the refusal to answer questions, so that the questor who is obliged to ask the two questions simultaneously can get no further and only enhances the silence by his persist-ence.

It is obvious that for the narrator of this story—

which Kafka wistfully called his *Bouvard and Pécuchet*:
'I'm writing rather prematurely my *Bouvard and
Pécuchet*'—his fellows' silence is most ominous in the
case of aerial dogs. It's an eloquent silence that fills the
void with insinuations, spreads over everything a mist
of uncontrollable possibilities and maintains canine
society in a state of superstitious gullibility by depriving it of reliable information. The first time he hears
about these improbable creatures he thinks it must be a
silly joke, and is furious anyone could imagine he
would be taken in:

> What? There is a species of very small dog, hardly bigger
> than my fist, not any bigger even when fully grown, and
> such constitutionally frail dogs—obviously unnatural
> and under-developed, groomed with exaggerated care,
> incapable of even leaping properly—such dogs, accord-
> ing to rumour, would spend the best part of their lives
> circling around very high up in the air, not by any means
> to perform some obvious function but, on the contrary,
> to relax? No, to my mind it is asking too much of a young
> pup's gullibility to expect me to believe such a thing.

But, since all the evidence tallies, the youthful sceptic
is converted. After the incident of the seven dog-
musicians which convinces him that nothing in this
world is too absurd or improbable to be possible, the
aerial dogs are given first priority in his investigations.

The humour of this improbable tale—which in fact
includes an authentic piece of autobiography—con-

sists in the contrast between a fantastic, unexpected name: aerial dogs, and the precise description of easily identifiable creatures. For the aerial dogs are mysterious only in name. In all other respects they are described with a meticulousness, precision and clarity worthy of the strictest scientific observation. (This is the case in all Kafka's stories where the seemingly fantastic derives from a gap between the vagueness of crucial words and the exact description of details. *The Trial* for instance, is only obscure because the word 'trial', used in a general sense, is both vague and charged with meaning. On the other hand everything that happens to Joseph K. is clear and coherent, so that if it were not for the spell cast by the key-word, readers would have no difficulty in following the ins and outs of the story). In these circumstances the symbol is misleading only when taken out of context because the reader then tries to decode the text instead of patiently reading on. However it immediately becomes functional once it is allowed to merge into the surrounding details where, in fact, everything is set out clearly and sequentially. Thus there is no end to the implications one could find in the term 'aerial dogs' (especially in the original where 'lufthunde' evokes in one word a number of equally acceptable notions, none of which, however, can claim to be an exclusively valid interpretation). Yet the peculiar occupation of these creatures in the midst, or more precisely above the heads of their fellows is not in doubt. (In the topsy-turvy world of Kafka's stories everything that is 'normally' expressed in words is expressed in silence). Indeed the Dog gives a detailed description of their occupation as well as of the reasons for his interest in them:

> Here as almost everywhere it isn't the accomplishment that worries me. It is wonderful, who could deny it, that these dogs should be able to fly in the sky, and I am ready to marvel at it with the rest. But what, to me, is much more surprising is the dumb absurdity of such an existence. As a rule no explanation is forthcoming, they float in the air and that's that, life goes on, every so often there is some talk of art and artists, no more. But why, good canine folk, why in the name of God do these dogs float? What does their occupation signify? Why can't we get a single word of explanation out of them? Why do they hover up there, allowing their paws, the pride of our race, to waste away far from mother earth, without sowing or reaping and, so it is said, abundantly fed besides at the expense of the canine race . . . ?

After this passage where the Dog enumerates his questions—he is very proud to have raised them even if they will never be answered—the satire develops naturally—or 'cynically' that is to say with 'doggy' impudence—around what is obviously the story's basic theme—art and the artist.

The aerial dogs stand for that special brand of art

which dwells in ivory towers high above the heads of ordinary folk who provide its daily bread, an art convinced of its superiority which it does not condescend to explain. As such they are 'artificial and immature' little monsters of egotism and conceit (they have 'excessively well-tended coats'). Besides having a delicate constitution that makes them unfit for exertions of any kind and reduces them to parasitism (they are apparently incapable even of sexual reproduction), their intellectual ability too is sadly impaired by the useless solitary lives they lead. According to the Dog—who admittedly only knows what he has been told by people who contemplate them from a distance and from below—there is nothing in their make-up to warrant either their reputation or the privileges they enjoy. In fact notwithstanding their capacity for make-believe, they are not themselves unaware of this and possibly even feel vaguely guilty, though this feeling, because of its vagueness, only enhances their frivolity:

They must contrive somehow or other—not overtly, of course, which would be against the rule of secrecy—to find an excuse for this kind of existence, or try at least to distract our attention so that it may pass unnoticed; which is what they apparently do by dint of practically unbearable verbosity. They always have something to tell us, now imparting the philosophical reflections in which they can, having renounced all physical activity, constantly indulge, and now the observations their

privileged position enables them to make. And despite
the fact that they are definitely not gifted with exceptionally lively minds—which is hardly surprising con-
sidering their dissolute lives; despite the fact that their
philosophy is as worthless as their observations and that
science, which anyhow has no truck with such pitiful
expedients, can put them to no use, every time you ask
what is the practical purpose of these flying dogs, you
will nonetheless be told that they contribute to the
advancement of learning. . . .

In short the aerial dogs who are physically misshapen,
and feebleminded into the bargain as a result of their
total isolation, are second-rate even where they claim
supremacy. Though their extreme verbosity somewhat disguises the shallowness of their minds, their
philosophical reflections, like their scientific observations are only remarkable for an amateurishness
consistent with their 'exalted station'—one and the
other are no more than idle chatter and of no earthly
use to philosophy or science. In the vacuum to which
their incurable conceit confines them the aerial dogs
are totally parasitic. With art as an excuse they are
kept by the community and live shamelessly at the
expense of science and philosophy to which they
contribute nothing of any value.

Such sponging and incompetence would be at least
tolerable if the exalted station from which these
degenerate creatures consider the world were a source

of inspiration. Unfortunately this is not the case. The aerial dogs have no message to transmit because, despite their angelic appearance, they are nobody's messengers and there are no messages of any kind to justify their peculiar existence. The narrator is quite explicit on the subject: there is nothing above or beyond the aerial dogs. It is a complete waste of time to question the heavens. They remain as silent and unresponsive as the flocks of shoddy angels in the clouds and as the earth from which our investigator seeks to extract its secrets. But:

> to who else can we appeal in the great void of this world? The whole of science, the sum total of questions and answers is contained in these dogs. . . .

So if there is no transcendent significance to the urge to float in the air, and if even the aerial dogs themselves have nothing to say about this urge, then their lofty art is mere affectation and fraud.

Though the satire is unambiguous it could doubtless be said that its object may be quite other than we have assumed. There is no proof that the aerial dogs' futile vocation is being satirised, rather than the narrow-mindedness of their critic for instance. Indeed the investigator cuts a rather poor figure in all this business. He is pedantic, niggling, over-confident and could easily stand for the limited, rationalistic academic or the philistine, naturally indifferent to fantasy and beauty. If such were the case the aerial dogs, far from depicting the triviality of a pointless, unproductive art, would stress instead the spiritual inadequacy of narrow-minded positivism founded on a meaningless universe deprived of all transcendence. The satire is then stood on its head. (This is how 'negative theology' operates: in the 'Investigations of a Dog' Kafka didn't try to express his own scepticism but was illustrating by means of this fable of a dog world deprived of man's presence, the distressing emptiness of a world without God). Such an interpretation is less easy to dismiss than might be supposed when applied to a form of narrative where significant elements are not assessed according to conventional norms. When Kafka conflates the contradictory images of the socially idealised questor and an animal usually epitomising lowliness and servility, does he want to denounce the dogginess of scholars or to suggest that animal instinct is precisely what is required for a greater spiritual understanding? Moreover of whom is he making fun in this dog world where, he assures us, original characters and strong personalities abound? Is he on the side of the Dog dedicated to scholarship, consumed by doubts and curiosity, totally impartial in his pursuit of the truth and who, as narrator, is automatically assumed to be his spokesman? Or in spite of everything is he defending his stunted, unproductive, aerial dog art against the censures of the incorruptible judge that was his conscience? No answer to such questions can be deduced from the word 'dog', although it is the key-word of the text. Indeed if Kafka had not dealt with the problem of art elsewhere it wouldn't be possible to decide whether the hero of this fable were his spokesman or not. But in fact all his major works are variations on the same theme and, since the fate of all his artists is more or less identical, there can be little doubt as to the pessimism of their creator's outlook.

Generally speaking, but more especially in his very last stories, Kafka depicts art as self-important, self-glorified and self-consuming, both germ and symptom of some agonising disease. But if in the Dog story there may be some doubt as to the object of his satire, in the later stories—'The Hunger Artist', 'Josephine the Singer, or the Mouse Folk'—there is no possibility of error. Between 1915 when Kafka wrote 'The Investigations of a Dog' and the two last artist-stories, written in 1922, which conclude his oeuvre, the pessimism of his satire becomes more and more ruthless till finally it turns upon its author to express itself in the most devastating statement of despair ever conceived.

The Hunger Artist, a virtuoso in the art of starvation, is no parasite like the aerial dogs and thus is spared their guilt-pangs. Indeed since his art consists precisely in starving, he can dispense simultaneously

with earning his living and with sponging on others.
(The tale's whole dialectic derives from the structure
of the word 'Hungerkünstler' where the conflation of
concepts suggests that hunger is an art, art an
unquenchable—or pathological—hunger and the
artist a starveling and thus the opposite of a plump
parasite. The juxtaposition of terms in the German
composite noun implies moreover that the artist uses
hunger as the means, aim and material of his creation.
He doesn't starve for the sake of creating but, on the
contrary, produces and exposes nothing else than his
own martyred flesh, thus making the absurdity of the
conclusion inevitable from the word go). However if
the Hunger Artist, who creates nothing but starvation,
can boast of depending on nobody, the public, on the
other hand, gets nothing out of his art which can
hardly be termed enlightening or inspiring. Though it
may briefly excite the curiosity of sensation-seekers,
all it has to offer is an exhibition of repulsive,
unwholesome gruesomeness which, being unmoti-
vated by practical necessity, moral obligation or
religious rites must remain totally incomprehensible
to all. (For the Hunger Artist, starving to death is a
completely disinterested art—indeed the only art that
can be seen as totally unconcerned with personal
benefit. But since he dies nonetheless in the end, his
staying-power is made void and meaningless unlike
that of the professional faster who deprives himself

within reason and in order to earn his daily bread). The Hunger Artist works for nobody's pleasure or profit. Self-consuming, living—or dying—off his own substance, he has nothing to communicate apart from the basic inhuman arrogance and complacency of his pointless asceticism. Hermit without a faith, ascetic without an order, martyr without a cause, even the perfection for which he strives is one more nail in his coffin. His utterly unproductive, objectless desire for perfection only succeeds in precipitating his final annihilation.

Because the Hunger Artist's art consists entirely in self-torture it can last precisely as long as the self has strength enough to inflict such torture. After which it vanishes, leaving the spectators—who rejoice at the sight of the now spotless cage occupied by a life-loving panther—with only the haziest recollection of its occurrence. The advent of the well-fed breast gleaming with health, irrefutable in its beauty and brute truth, welcomed by the public with shouts of joy, marks the end of an era's extended agony—an era where art was in the way of becoming a near-substitute for religion. To Kafka, hopelessly consumed by this surrogate faith, such a death is not to be lamented since he suspected that the starveling art to which he had sacrificed everything was ultimately a delusion. Thus the world —to which anyhow the Hunger Artist had never had anything to say—will certainly be none the worse for the disappearance, shortly to follow that of the artist himself, of the faith by which he had lived exclusively and to so little purpose. It will record the fact with its usual indifference, and there will be no repercussions. The death of an illusion, however heartbreaking it may be for the deluded, is really not a tragedy. On the contrary, it is rather comforting. That is why the Hunger Artist vanishes unobtrusively, of his own accord—or as Kafka puts it in the last of his stories: 'joyfully'.

Josephine, the Mouse Folk's *national* singer, has more dignity and poise than either the aerial dogs or the Hunger Artist imprisoned behind the bars of his obsession. She has the advantage over these representatives of an extravagant, absurdly isolated, unrealistic art, of being well ensconced in a clearly defined community where she even enjoys a certain status. Opinions may differ as to the actual quality of her voice or the social significance of her recitals, but Josephine doesn't sing for her own pleasure nor in the pursuit of a problematic ideal: she sings for an audience. This fact distinguishes her radically from the antisocial, rootless creatures who suffer or vegetate without rhyme or reason in Kafka's fables about the solipsistic, self-centred artist's private Inferno. Josephine suffers neither from the Dog's morbid curiosity nor from the Hunger Artist's fatal asceticism. Indifferent to the interior motives of her vocation as to the intrinsic value of her talent, her scope in life is to obtain absolute recognition and admiration from her fellows—incidentally the only absolute to which she is capable of aspiring. Thus the satire, aimed here at the hackneyed romantic idea of the eternal conflict between the artist and society—is set on a more realistic level than either of the others.

The Mouse Folk never asked Josephine to sing. It was her idea and she does so when she feels like it—the others simply accept the fact without bothering to refute or to confirm her self-appointed qualifications. This is really a comic version of the tragic predicament in which Kafka's Land Surveyor finds himself in *The Castle* (for his misfortune: he would have been so much better off could he have evaded it!). K., who arrives in the village as the officially appointed Land Surveyor, learns that the Castle has not been notified of any such appointment. Later, seeing that he will leave no stone unturned in his efforts to vindicate his right to the title and that he cannot be deterred from his purpose, the Castle authorities appear to think better of it, and the 10th Bureau, after allocating two 'assistants' to his service, unofficially informs him that he has given satisfaction and invites him to carry on (doing what, it is hard to tell, since K. has not started and will never start to do anything). Owing to a basic flaw in the symbolic interpretations of this novel, the conflicting messages from the Castle are imputed, not indeed to a pack of lies, but to a systematic deception intended to enlighten K.—or Man straying in the maze of wordly ways—on the vanity of trying to fathom the Divine Scheme with his own limited understanding. It is quite amazing that anyone should ascribe to Kafka such theological platitudes, especially as there is no suggestion anywhere in the text of deception, whether systematic or otherwise. Indeed it is made perfectly clear on both occasions that the Castle acts and speaks truthfully. In the first place on hearing that K. has assumed the role of Land Surveyor, the authorities inform him simply and sincerely that they have no knowledge of his nomination (Kafka uses the term: *Berufung*, which means vocation), but that he is otherwise free to do as he likes. However, when K., ignoring their message, persists in trying to carry out his plan and shows by his unusual tenacity a total dedication to the idea of practising his profession, the Castle authorities automatically acknowledge the fact in an unofficial message. This is not to say that the reality of K.'s vocation is acknowledged, but only his untiring efforts to make the world accept it. If K. wants to assume the title of qualified Land Surveyor and if his predicament is made absurd not to say hopeless by his persistence in pursuing this vocation after he has been told that his services are not required, well and good. Such perseverance is worthy of respect—and public opinion does in fact respect it without either assessing its intrinsic value or attempting to discourage him further. For the collective organism whose conscious power and unconscious reactions—or practical rationality and impulsive desires—are both embodied in the Castle, is not competent to decide whether K. has really been called as he says he has, or whether he is labouring under a delusion. This organism is essentially passive and capable neither of positively dissuading him nor of confirming the reality of his purpose. As the villagers assert, it would be childish or insane to believe otherwise and to try and obtain public recognition of an entirely private undertaking. But K. is quite incorrigible (he persists in seeing Barnabas as an 'official' messenger, rather than recognising that the youth to whom he entrusts his 'papers' is a reflection of his own perpetually uncorroborated vocation). Since he won't tolerate arbitrariness—the one law which governs art and inspiration—he dies exhausted by superhuman, pointless efforts before he has had a chance to start working and without even knowing what he might have achieved had he only been able to dispense with the world's blessings.

In this respect Josephine is less ambitious. She isn't interested in absolutes, nor has she any of K.'s disturbing scruples about the authenticity of her vocation. (True, K's scruples didn't stop him from seeking public sanction for a vocation he wasn't sure of possessing). Josephine doesn't care whether she has a warrant or not. She sings because she wants to be acknowledged as a singer. And in practice, if not in principle, she is acknowledged as such, whatever doubts the public may have as to the quality of her talent.

In fact Josephine's attitude conforms to the Castle conventions that Frieda tries so hard to make K. understand: the Gentlemen don't meddle with private decisions. The people 'from here', unlike the foreign Land Surveyor, know this perfectly well. Therefore they don't expect to have their wives chosen for them by the authorities, but get married when and to whom they want. Josephine is unquestionably 'from here' and not from the improbable elsewhere whence aerial dogs and Hunger Artists come. Thus she practises her art without a thought for the Gentlemen's acknowledgement, and the Gentlemen let her sing in view of the law stipulating that an existing vocation should be automatically tolerated as such. This law, common to every society and ignored by K. at his peril, is naturally in force among the Mouse Folk who submit without demur to Josephine's claim to fame. However they are not expected to concede more than passive acceptance and are not obliged to pander to her need for consecration. Whence the rift that gradually widens between the singer and her audience, and the painful alternative of the title (Josephine the Singer *or* the Mouse Folk) which the latter have no qualms in settling.

Josephine is predictably not content with her accommodating audience's benevolent neutrality. She wants more. She requires and expects constant adulation, a total understanding of her art's most subtle nuances and the ecstatic gratitude of her fellow mice—for all of which she affects, however, the utmost contempt. But the Mouse Folk are quite fond of Josephine and they are prepared to go a long way to please her. They flock to her recitals and are ready to humour her up to a point. But they don't take her threats seriously and furthermore they refuse to be put upon, especially as a large proportion of her audience (including the narrator) is not even convinced of her talent. They sometimes wonder if it is art at all, if it is even singing:

> Isn't it rather a mere piping? We all know what piping is, it's the peculiar talent of our folk, or rather it's not even a talent but a racial character. We all pipe without anybody obviously thinking of it as an art, without thinking about it, without noticing . . . Could it be that Josephine doesn't sing but merely pipes? And could it even be (at least that's my impression) that she doesn't pipe any differently from anybody else? (All in all I tend to believe that she isn't capable of piping fluently, while the merest navvy does it effortlessly all day as he goes on working). In this case Josephine's art doesn't exist but

this only makes it harder to explain the mystery of her enormous impact . . .

Thus the most readily accepted art—which is also the healthiest in Kafka's view—is nothing but an imitation of a people's natural talent and its whole impact derives from the simple fact that it can afford a whole range of props and sets which the piping toiler can't— even were he to appreciate their advantage. Art's impact is not intrinsic but depends mainly on the pomp and circumstance surrounding its exhibitions. In other words on the almighty cheek of an artist who summons crowds from far and wide to witness a trifling performance, an ordinary gesture which anyone can do just as well anywhere and at any time.

> Even if we were dealing with an ordinary piping the matter should still present the oddity of showing someone who takes a firm stand in order to do nothing out of the ordinary. Nut-cracking is certainly not an art and no one, in consequence, would dare summon an audience to amuse it by cracking nuts. Were he to do so, however, and were his initiative crowned with success, it would mean that it was really something other than a simple question of cracking nuts. Or if it were a simple question of cracking nuts, it would mean that we had never considered such an art because we had mastered it completely and that the new nut-cracker had revealed its true essence, in which case it might even be required that he be a little less skilful at it than us . . .

So the mystery of art is reduced to a *Kunststück* (a conjuring trick: 'K. was a great conjuror . . . ' says Kafka in an unfinished fragment), or such an artless fraud that no one takes the trouble to expose it. Art isn't the product of lofty inspiration but of an illusion the artist creates by advertising his intention to create—if so many people gather to see the nothing I see, this nothing must surely conceal something remarkable, or at least be loaded with unsuspected significance, otherwise why these crowds, and not a titter to be heard? The miracle of art, the *Kunststück*, isn't the result of a mysterious spiritual process as its exhibitions would suggest, but depends almost entirely on the colossal impudence of an individual who claims and obtains the public's undivided and admiring attention for his handling of an ordinary nut-cracker.

Kafka's artist may be an empty wind-bag like the aerial dogs or in deadly earnest like the Hunger Artist, but he is always entirely self-motivated, and the arbitrariness of his self-begetting is proof both of his self-sufficiency—he is sufficient unto himself and unto all—and of his total irresponsibility. Sacred and self-consecrated, he makes his mark thanks to his own unshakable faith in the reality of his talent—a faith he communicates, not as private belief, but as objective, undeniable truth. His persuasiveness allows him to enjoy—with public gratitude and approval—an un-equalled position, while his congenital stigmas are

either ignored or seen as evidence of predestina-
tion.

Since the artist's physical strength has been
neglected in favour of his intellectual conceit, he must
try to compensate for what his feeble constitution
cannot procure him. Thus while his depravity of mind
increases his physical inadequacy, this inadequacy
tends to enhance his despotism. Physically handicapped and mentally puerile, not to say infantile, he
skilfully exploits his weaknesses to avoid social obliga-
tions. And the total exemption he demands, quite
apart from its practical advantage, implicitly vindi-
cates his most extravagant claims (I demand so much
from you because my art is your salvation and my
demands are proof of my rights).

Such an attitude is responsible for the minor conflict
between Josephine and the long-suffering mice. They
are willing to pamper their national star who is so
vulnerable under her inspired airs. But they can't give
in to all her whims. She must abide by the laws of the
community or quit the scene together with her art and
her personal problems. Josephine never tires of ex-
plaining that she is much more than a simple enter-
tainer. Do not the Mouse Folk owe her their very lives
since it is she who unites and encourages them in times
of stress and gives them the necessary strength to
struggle on? This feeble little creature with barely
strength enough to sing (at times even that is too much

for her—or so she says), doesn't hesitate to play the Saviour, the bringer of new strength to her suffering people. How then can they be so ungrateful as to grudge her the preferential treatment that is essential to her creativity? Such an argument carries some weight when addressed to a population threatened on all sides by fearful and ruthless enemies. Josephine's chronicler admits as much. He even goes on to say that her claims are not altogether unfounded:

> Doubtless she doesn't save us or encourage us; it is only too easy to set oneself up as the savior of our people(. . .) which has always more or less saved itself, were it at the price of sacrifices before which historians (. . .) are struck dumb; it would seem that at such moments we swallow at one gulp—yes, there is no time to lose, and Josephine too often forgets it—a last cup of peace before the battle. It isn't so much a concert, then, as a public gathering, a gathering where the silence is total—save for a tiny piping voice.

Of course Josephine will have no truck with an explanation that belittles rather than exalts the significance of her art. She wants to inspire heroic deeds and not, as her spiteful chronicler suggests, promote a welcome drowsiness before the inevitable call to action. And so she does, say her supporters:

> or how can we account for the popularity of her concerts, at the most critical moments which, indeed,

has often prevented us from taking steps to avoid the danger?

That's what proves her wrong, say her detractors, for the gatherings she promotes provide the enemy with ideal conditions for a surprise attack, after which she;

> who is responsible for it all and has perhaps attracted the enemy's attention by her piping, is the first to depart on the quiet under her escort's protective wing . . .

Such controversies might drag on for ever if the public, ignorant of such niceties, did not, one fine day, take justice into its own hands.

But it is Josephine who brings things to a head by over-stepping the limits of presumption. The prerogatives she enjoys are no longer enough:

> she wants to be exempted from work of any kind; she should be relieved of the worry of having to earn her daily bread and of the duties involved in our struggle for life, which means that the population as a whole would have to assume them.

Thus she resorts to the sort of overweening assertion that most impresses art's devotees. For who would presume to live officially at the expense of the community if he were not convinced that he was paying for such material sacrifice in priceless spiritual benefits to that community? Alas, the more an artist *presumes* so much more is it *presumed* that such is his right as creator and dispenser of fabulous riches that can never be requited in material goods, and are therefore literally priceless. Romantic notions of inspiration have turned such presumptions into reality, and no one knows better than Josephine how to exploit them. But although there are what the chronicler calls 'the facile enthusiasts', who are only too willing to be taken in, the population as a whole is resolute. It recognises no saviour to whom it is indebted and will give as much as it intended to give and no more. Nobody, however exceptional his gifts, will make it change its mind.

Josephine argues and complains, threatens to cut short her grace-notes or to report sick. But all to no avail. Sick or not, fit or unfit Josephine must work for her daily bread. Such is the law and it knows no exception. But Josephine can't and won't give in. To accept the general verdict would be to admit that her presumptions are founded on conceit, and that would be the end of her since her artistic career depends on the sharing of her presumptions. There is nothing left for her to do but retire from public life:

> She is in hiding and sings no more, but the people, who keep quiet and don't express their disappointment, this people, supreme master who can only give and never receive, even from Josephine the Singer, despite all evidence to the contrary, this people simply carries on.

Josephine is finally beaten because she wants to justify

her idleness by playing the part of historical saviour. She falls into her own trap, believing she is strong enough to stand alone against society. In fact all she can do is to provoke and annoy the public and so hasten her downfall:

> Josephine can only deteriorate. The day will soon come when her last breath will have expired. She is only an insignificant incident in the eternal history of our people and our people will overcome their loss . . .

A sad end, perhaps, but Josephine, even defeated is better off than the solitary zealots to whom Kafka allots the extreme severity of his own fate. Living among her fellows and singing for them she avoids the Hunger Artist's horrible death: without kin or country or a History in which to 'happily' lose himself, he leaves only a repulsive memory of foolish pride and rotting flesh. Josephine too will die, of course, and she too will not have revolutionised the world, but her end is not entirely without hope, for her kinsfolk are not resentful by nature and once she has learnt her lesson they will welcome her back to the fold. Then she will 'happily lose herself in the numberless throng of the heroes of her people' and, like her brothers, slowly sink into oblivion.

In the mirror Kafka holds up to the literature of his age—and he is entitled to do so since he never tired of seeing and judging himself in it—the artist lives in a nightmare expressly created to dispel all the airy-fairy notions the word 'art' traditionally conjures up. Yet the reflections in this wilfully distorting mirror are not caricatures. Grotesque and exaggerated perhaps, they are nonetheless realistic in so far as they portray accurately the *negative* our cultural conventionalists make it their job to conceal (as a rule, says Kafka, 'we must create the negative, the positive has already been provided.'). Thus the portion of reality carefully concealed under all our talk about art is boldly exposed in each of these figures. But they have a further purpose—while deflating the forced optimism of official discourse, they simultaneously provide the author himself with a means of trying out new solutions and allowing his creative experience to develop freely according to the laws of its own logic. K. the Land Surveyor, the Trapeze Artist, Josephine or the Hunger Artist, to name the most obvious, illustrate in their various experiences the inner conflict an artistic vocation involves. In each case there is the chance of a fresh start in more favourable conditions, and thus the possibility of finding the right answer. In other words the real artist is asking the fictional artist to help him understand what his faith in art is all about. Is it worth the price he has to pay or is it only the fabrication of a diseased mind? We already know the answer: it is a dumb-show, since the fictional artist is dumb by definition, but it is an unambiguous picture of

total failure and unpardonable error. And since
Kafka's artist tales were all written just before his
death and since, by a remarkable exception, he wanted
them to be published, it may be seen as his personal
testament.

All the fictional artists who act out their calvary
before their author's eyes bear the same congenital
stigma, and therefore, naturally enough, they are all
prone to the same disease. Of course there are
anecdotal variants—they are men or beasts, they
inhabit an identifiable environment or a world of pure
fantasy—as well as more serious differences due to the
proportion and distribution of their common char-
acteristics. These—magnified in some, toned down in
others or combined with less fatal ingredients—are
symptoms of the true cause of their sickness—the
childishness responsible both for their incapacity to
cope with life and for the nature of their vocation. The
positive which current ethics might concede to them,
like the negative with which they are generously
provided, stems from a basic unfitness due to chronic
immaturity. They are incredibly childish, a mixture of
weakness and excess, pride and impotence, depend-
ence and desire for freedom—the Trapeze Artist sobs
on his manager's shoulder for a second trapeze,
obviously convinced that one more apparatus will
make all the difference. In short they can't win—
eternally childish, incapable of ever growing up

because they turn their weakness into despotism, their greatest gifts are precisely those which are their undoing.

Thus the Romantic illusion crumbles away on all sides under the piercing gaze of the writer whom literature most utterly possessed—in the truly demonic sense—and as it collapses, the real questions can at last be asked. Since Kafka was, in his own words, nothing but literature, he obviously starts by attacking himself, not as one tends to believe, for the sake of morbid self-destruction and self-mockery, but because the excess and misuse of literature positively stopped him from writing. Illusion must be eradicated where it is most deeply rooted. There is no other solution if literature is not to be left in mid-air, lost between a paradise of narcissistic exaggeration and the world where it has no foothold. Such purposeful demythologising requires the impersonal style of an official report oblivious of aesthetic controversy as of every kind of ideology. (Needless to say, it will satisfy the philistine and the zealot no more than the idealist— indeed it will satisfy nobody who is not prepared to make an exceptional effort, since it attacks all the categories into which our concepts are classified.) Neither positive nor negative but indispensable as the one remedy that can save literature, it is the uprooted artist's last stand against the myth an outdated tradition maintains to conceal its puerile shortcomings and excesses, its frivolous exploitation of the absolute, its selfishness and its perversity. In this respect demythologising is modernity's last chance, or at least its only legitimate source of inspiration.

*

But perhaps things have changed and the disease—if so positive a term can be applied to such an imprecise phenomenon—from which we suffer today bears no relation to Kafka's demonic possession. True the Trapeze Artist and the Hunger Artist have vanished without trace from the circus—where nobody is going to miss them. Contented, if not happy people have replaced them, self-assured, self-satisfied people confident in their potentialities and the value of their 'spontaneous' fantasies. They have no use for art, learning, effort or of course for craftsmanship, but genius can be had for the asking, the free gift, freedom—so why should anybody suffer anguish, torment and self-doubt? In a world where the 'torments of creation' can only be mentioned between inverted commas the crazy Hunger Artist is so totally alien that no one is likely to rack his brains over his predicament. On the other hand aerial dogs and singing mice have every chance of success—they are all over the place and make the head-lines. They have never been so bold nor has their chatter and piping ever been greeted with such acclaim—this is the one positive achievement in the great wave of confusion that bears them on high and for which they are mainly responsible.

*

Megalomania of the Novel. In a press review (where it passed unnoticed among more sensational items) Solzhenitsyn declared that the novel isn't merely a means of expression but a revealer of Truth, no less. The novelist's depth and precision of inner perception sets him above historians and scientists who, as everybody knows, are blinkered and totally deprived of the inspired, all-embracing vision required to re-create events as they actually occurred. Where the expert gropes blindly for fragments, the prophetic, far-sighted novelist can judge History rather than be judged by it. (This is an approximate rendering of Solzhenitsyn's words which I failed to take down at the time.) Such faith in the novel's power is only to be expected from someone who believes he can move an empire with his writings. Indeed it's what makes the struggle possible and may even ensure the success of the whole unrealistic enterprise. But that isn't the point. What amazes me is that at a time when the novel's reputation is in many respects decidedly on the wane it should continue to assert its unrivalled power and far-sightedness. Though in Solzhenitsyn's world human relationships, living conditions and the foundations of knowledge have undergone a radical change, he is just as confident in the powers of magic as were his great predecessors. Like Balzac he sees himself as 'History's secretary', or like Zola as 'Humanity's examining magistrate' (and what is more, such magic may really be effective, though no one can say for how long).

*

Whenever I pass the *Hotel des Invalides*—which is quite often since I live just round the corner—I wonder how it would have been planned and built if the term 'Invalides' (disabled) had been proscribed from the official vocabulary at the time. I don't want to suggest a mysterious correspondence between architecture and our conventional social reticence, but surely our extraordinary linguistic acrobatics inspired by human respect must influence our artefacts and what little style we have. However, whether we acknowledge or not our fear of words and the barbarisms to which it gives rise, paupers, old people, savages and cripples have definitely ceased to exist. Instead we have the economically underprivileged, senior citizens, under-developed countries and the handicapped—which may relieve our social conscience but does very little to assist those concerned. Since we can't rid the world of its misery we exclude from our vocabulary the destitute, the maids-of-all-work and the good-for-nothings who formerly bore the stigmas of inferiority, deficiency and degeneracy—though we haven't yet quite succeeded in sweeping the sick and the dead under the carpet—they are altogether a tougher proposition. In fact we try to disguise the seamy side of mere existence by refusing to use all the words that spell it out and replacing them by more seemly terms. If such substitutions are an indication of the complexity of our motives for human respect, they also stress the fact that words for us are magically invested with the properties of their content—that they are superstitious cult-objects. We believe they can unloose or, perhaps more rarely, restrain the active powers they innocently signify. Contrary to linguistic theories (which I shall not discuss here) we can't be dissuaded from our conviction that the word 'dog' bites and might become rabid. Thus the mention of paupers involves a twofold risk—such a rash allusion to the Powers of Wealth could provoke the unfavoured to rebellion as well as offend the wealthy by confronting them with evidence of their privileges. Whence the compound 'economically underprivileged' which is too weak and spineless to be dangerous.

But are we really so misguided in abiding, despite

logic and theory, by the laws of primitive magic? Though our clumsy euphemisms may do more to disguise than to cure, at least the underprivileged are spared the added humiliation of their former titles. And if they did nothing else they would still be worth more than charitable well-wishing. For while they don't, of course, cancel out the past by simply declaring that it is over, they do spotlight the new leaf we would so much like to turn over. Besides, though it's difficult if not impossible to judge the extent of their influence on our manners and minds, in the long run they may perhaps contribute as much to social ethics as they have certainly detracted from language and aesthetics (which are responsible for the process and must thus pay for its success). But what exactly do 'perhaps' and 'certainly' mean in this context? Today's 'home help' can never on any account find herself immortalised in a book like the simple-hearted Feli-citée (Flaubert's *Un Coeur simple*). But is that impor-tant, after all, compared to what the euphemism's implicit censure of servility may perhaps achieve? The loss of simple hearts to come probably distresses precisely those who most sincerely abhor servility— and such a loss is indeed distressing in its restricted field but quite insignificant in the context of real life, since whatever it means to us its only significance is in the books where real people's accounts are not entered.

*

More about our fear of words.—When I was a little girl I was much taken by a cheap colour-print hanging above my parents' bed. It was one of those still lives where crusty loaves and sparkling decanters flank the inevitable hare or pheasant. But oddly enough what most intrigued me wasn't the animal—though an animal thus suspended between life and death should have distressed me—but a commonplace drinking vessel whose size and shape didn't correspond to my notions of such objects (I'd never seen one like it). Not that I was afraid of this truly 'unheimlich' object, familiar and yet unknown. It simply aroused my curiosity as something that didn't fit in to any category, something unclassifiable. However when my mother told me it was a beaker the word had an effect the visible image had failed to produce. I was seized with such terror and screamed so loud and long that my mother was hard put to console me. Equipped with a beak (which I naturally took literally) as no honest drinking vessel should be, the thing had become a monstrous hybrid, half object and half bird, capable of flying at me and pecking me savagely. The dread this word had inspired gradually subsided after I had realised that, beaked or not, the thing wasn't dangerous to look at (actually, I suspect that my fear wasn't really aroused by the goblet at all but rather by the pheasant I was trying to ignore because its embellished corpse, still warm and palpitating under its bright feathers, embodied all the horror of something neither quite alive nor quite dead far more vividly than the beaker).

*

Against all odds the novel-as-message is still thriving. Thus when Professor Barnard's novel was published he declared to the press: 'The novel form seemed the most suitable in which to express my ideas on medicine. The pen is mightier than the scalpel in many respects.' One might think that the famous surgeon doesn't have a very high opinion of his profession and shows little gratitude to his scalpel (whose fame will doubtless enhance that of his modest pen). Moreover if he has any professional opinions, those he expresses about their literary medium—not to mention his apparent scorn for patients and readers alike—won't help to make them very popular. But the ineptitude of such a remark is nonetheless revealing as one more example of the way in which literature is generally overrated since, even when a man has attained success in another field, he still hankers after the writer's laurels as if nothing else could satisfy his megalomania.

*

A journalist (Jean Lacouture) contrasts in an article the Khmer Rouge's vehemence with the level-headedness of Vietnamese revolutionaries. Thus we are presented with a picture of a slightly overheated conversation involving people of different temperaments—some vehement and some level-headed—each behaving characteristically and neither faction being intrinsically better or worse than the other, so that our personal sympathies are a simple question of taste. Moreover the whole thing is purely a matter of common psychology and isn't anything to make a fuss about, nor is it of any historical importance.

But we gradually realise that it is in fact far more significant and complex than the tone of the article had at first led us to suppose. Because first of all it isn't just a matter of 'contrast' but equally of 'parallelism' between two attitudes which remain similar despite their antynomy (vehemence and level-headedness are opposed everywhere except in this particular case where they follow a parallel course). Further we are informed that it has nothing to do with psychology but with political sociology for which, moreover, 'it can't fail to become an issue.' So now all is clear: the terms we had taken for definitions of two ways of expressing affectivity, or two typically national attitudes, really define two means of assuming power, two temporarily divergent tactics ultimately achieving the same end. Thus 'vehemence' was used to avoid saying 'violence', 'level-headedness' followed only so as to suggest a peaceful discussion while avoiding 'moderation' which might have seemed exaggerated, and 'parallel' qualified 'contrast' to dispel any idea of antagonism between the two terms of the comparison. Incidentally I must confess that, accustomed as I am to automatically adjusting tendentious euphemisms, I had already understood what it was all about.

*

Perplexity of teachers of French at the Luchon conference. According to one of the participants as reported in *le Monde*, teachers of French are in a state of 'genuine confusion concerning the meaning and even the purpose (sic) of their discipline.' Indeed what could be more disturbing than to teach a subject whose meaning is unclear and which furthermore has no precise purpose? (To judge by the wording of the phrase it seems that there might be some point in teaching a totally meaningless subject so long as it had a purpose of some kind.) The teachers' spokesman is obviously sincere—the tone of the statement is proof of his perplexity—but really, why should anyone want to teach something he hasn't even bothered to learn himself?

*

The crucial role of the translator in introducing foreign literatures and especially in spreading and modifying ideas, is rarely given its due. If the Bible hadn't been read in other tongues and in other countries than those of its origins what impact would it have had? Indeed there isn't a religion, doctrine or discovery which doesn't owe its fame and endurance to translation. Christianity, Marxism, Freudianism—to mention only the more widely acknowledged—could hardly have achieved their present ascendancy had not generations of interpreters made available beyond the narrow boundaries of their native lands the books through which they were first divulged. In this respect the translator isn't just the proverbial traitor—he creates at least as much as he betrays, since ideas couldn't conquer the world without his intervention. In fact even his worst betrayals are creative and the doctrines he transmits never reach their destination without a certain amount of modification, so that a large proportion have only triumphed thanks to his incompetence, artlessness, pious zeal or deliberate apologetical bias.

Whether it is through carelessness, ignorance or ideological faith, translations are rarely more than an uneasy compound of error and authenticity, and any authority they may achieve is usually based on complex, often improbable and anachronistic interpretations of the more impenetrable passages.

Naturally enough it is the classical texts, both sacred and profane, which suffer most from such clumsy or overskilful and 'inspired' counterfeits. But if the modern writer is more accessible, he nonetheless fares no better. Though his contemporaries may be technically equipped to convey his meaning faithfully they are no less prone to the temptation which besets all translators to make a text say what they want it to say. Thus their misinterpretations could be seen almost as 'Freudian slips'.

For instance when theological interpretations of Kafka were all the rage even the simplest word in the most obvious context could not be allowed to indicate what it stood for since it came from a pen that was exclusively at the service of lofty ideas. When Kafka mentioned in his *Journal* that Rudolf Steiner the famous anthroposophist, was never without a 'Kerze' in his pocket, French translators called it a 'cierge' (votive candle) rather than 'bougie' (the ordinary candle it was) which they considered too commonplace to be possible. Yet just a couple of lines later Kafka explains—not without a trace of mischievous humour —that Dr Steiner was inseparable from his candle-end because he was inordinately afraid of the dark and dreaded black-outs more than anything else. Obviously we are none of us entirely immune from such moments of aberration when culture and common-sense both cease to function. But the point is not that anyone can sometimes be mistaken, but the awe-inspiring, almost blinding effect of similar misinterpretations which, because they are convincing and because they are rarely corrected, only consolidate the tendencies which inspired them.

But although the etymological synonymy of 'translation' and 'interpretation' still holds (witness the works by French Freudians in the last fifteen years where exegesis defines the meaning of words which in turn gives rise to further commentary) the unintentional or tendentious adulteration of texts is not always detrimental—indeed a number of works would probably have been far less successful if they had been correctly translated, and it has certainly been largely responsible for the popularisation of innumerable spiritual trends (so-called profane or lay Old Testament criticism has gradually uncovered an infinity of unintentional misinterpretations in the Septuagint which have been more or less wittingly exploited apologetically in the New Testament and later used as proof and basis for the more impenetrable points of dogma—to no avail, it would seem, since the Sacred Texts have lost none of their authority nor, for the faithful, of their inspired quality). When one thinks of the enormous disproportion between the original slip and its consequences, one feels that the most appealing undertaking imaginable would be to rewrite the history of ideas from this angle.

*

A good book affects us through objects which only exist in a particular association of words and which are not intended to arouse any feeling of covetousness. A bad book, on the contrary, affects us by means of crude images representing tangible, consumable things particularly apt to arouse desire (thrillers, detective stories and erotic fiction, whose ostentatious purpose is to excite physical desire and passion, belong to the second category whether the author likes it or not). Yet on second thoughts I have to admit that the distinction is not always so clear-cut as to provide a hard-and-fast rule, for even the best books sometimes include aesthetically questionable passages which stimulate enthusiasm pure and simple rather than literary enthusiasm (passages which make us exclaim: How true!)—Needless to say, Madame Bovary's clothes don't interest me in the least as things to be worn, yet I have sometimes caught myself dreaming about the extraordinary hair-styles she invents both to change her face and to dispel boredom (it's true that every reader is subject to moments of shallowness just as every author can be caught off his guard; yet *The Sentimental Education* contains nothing that could be put to such use). So I simply can't understand why, for me, Madame Bovary's hair-styles should fall short of literature and still less do I understand the pleasure I derive from a 'Black Series'* hero sitting down to a hearty breakfast after a night of seduction and crime. Yet the twelve-egg omelette, the pile of griddle cakes dripping with maple syrup and the pot of steaming black coffee which have nothing to do with literature and would make me sick in real life are terribly tempting in such a context.

*

Paradoxically, though to me not entirely illogically, I tend to believe that what I find so appealing in that unassuming 'Black Series' breakfast is precisely what I have always disliked in Proust's madeleine.

*

'Illustrations are anti-literary' Flaubert said indignantly when his publisher Charpentier wanted to bring out an illustrated edition of one of his books: 'Do you want any old fool to depict what I have taken such pains *not to show*?' And though Kafka had to resign himself to the fact that Kurt Wolff would put a picture on the cover of the *Metamorphosis* since such was the publisher's policy for the collection in which it

---

* A French series of popular detective stories, similar to Penguin 'greenbacks'.

appeared, he begged him to make sure that at least the insect would not be represented: 'Not that, please not that!' (In fact he was spared 'that' since on the cover of the *Princeps* edition Gregory is shown as a man standing alone in an empty room, his back to a door half open on darkness and his face buried in his hands).

But whether the prospect of having his works illustrated provokes anger or dread in the author, such reactions are never the expression of a passing whim. They reflect any *consistent* writer's attitude to the modern craze for mixing arts and styles. For Flaubert and Kafka—both modern enough in their time but quite uncompromising where their art was concerned —the first principle of all art is inner consistency within the precise limits of its particular style where transpositions of any kind are impossible. Literary images can't be translated into visual images because they only exist in the space and time of a given verbal organisation and not in their seemingly transposable elements which are precisely what writing must overcome. (Flaubert takes such pains not to show what he describes.) Thus the quality of added or substituted images is immaterial: such images must be avoided for the simple reason that the thing seen destroys the written thing by representing it. (Even Jean Renoir's 'Madame Bovary' would have distressed Flaubert, and Kafka's reaction to the proliferation of plays and films produced in his name doesn't bear thinking about.)

*

J. L. Curtis asserts in *Questions à la litérature* that existentialism is to be thanked—or blamed, according to the point of view—for the fact that 'literary freedom is a thing of the past.' Really? Is there now a law to define and ratify literary crimes and a special law court to ensure its application? It seems though, that apart from the odd ideological censure of writers committed to the wrong cause—not to mention of course the real trials which are not immediately concerned with literary issues—if books are frequently appreciated for their 'message', they are not within the province of law and order so that, as far as literature is concerned, a writer is free to use or misuse language to his own ends with total impunity. He is entitled to make unsubstantiated assertions, to settle matters he is not qualified to settle, to contradict himself and generally to believe that what he wants to be true is in fact true—all of which is part of his job. He can cheat, lie, misjudge and withal play the part of a master-thinker while his shortcomings, illusions and inconsistencies are never held against him by posterity any more than by his contemporaries. Since there exists no legal authority competent to judge him nobody dares even to record them.

*

When I was at the so-called 'Oedipal' age, few things fascinated me more than 'word families' and everything that was vaguely connected with them. I was thrilled by the idea that words could give birth to other words and thus constitute something very similar to human families, and my discovery of this peculiarity promptly turned my studies into a game (I enjoyed playing with derived or compound words more than with any toy). However there was more to it than that for my interest stemmed from subtler causes and long-forgotten fears. The human family appeared to be a haphazard affair or at best based on unknown, intriguing and equivocal laws, whereas word-families had nothing to hide and derived from clearly defined rules easily learnt and applied which I was not only allowed to investigate, but positively encouraged to do so. Moreover since meaning replaced blood in their kinship, they were immediately intelligible and at the same time elevated to a rarified atmosphere where all the mystery and murkiness of family promiscuity played no part. Words were born like children, yet their birth was not surrounded by secrecy—which made all the difference. They were generated in broad daylight by simply appending a prefix or a suffix to the parent root—a wonderful method that presented the double advantage of making learning easier (one word could yield ten) and of removing from the real family all its puzzling, or even terrifying aspects. Thus procreation, thanks to grammar, was promoted from a carnal to an intellectual process, and it thus became entirely licit to take an interest in it since words, while coming delightfully close to the forbidden subject, provided the best protection against transgression. At last there was no risk in playing with fire—reality could be recreated without guilt.

*

The dilemma of the 'I' who says 'If I am not for myself who will be for me? And if I am for myself who am I?' (Talmud)—That is what Valéry's *Ego Scriptor* can't solve.

*

'He was capable of covering a hundred pages yet incapable of inventing a language for his hundred unwritten pages.'—Karl Kraus' apt critique of Heine loses some of its exemplary value when we think of the number of living or dead writers to whom it might apply.

*

I am taken aback to find that Balzac, in *la Femme Auteur*, talks of 'a free-thinking, Voltairian, not to say slightly communist husband . . . '. A communist in Balzac? In 1830? Can it be possible? This currently topical term seems so out of place and incongruous here that I was, at first, sure I had misread it. However its history is common knowledge as well as the fact that it was already currently used in Balzac's day. Nonetheless it is surprising to come across it in this unexpected context, perhaps precisely because of its remarkable familiarity. For if its meaning has barely changed over the years it evokes today an endless sequence of events, achievements, dates, names and images with which it is intricately related in our minds but which Balzac obviously knew nothing of.

*

Fragment of a dream.—In reply to some complaint my interlocuter says: 'We must have some esculapus.' I take this word, pronounced with an unexpected initial aspiration, as an incitement to courage or hope or perhaps both—hope of recovery and courage to carry on. But owing to the characteristic ambiguity of dream neologisms (they are always droll and basically aggressive) I am aware at the same time that it involves an urge to give in. (In this case the ambiguity is based on reality: it derives from the two plaster busts to be found in the drug-store I usually go to, one of peaceful, delicate featured, curly headed Esculapus, the other of Hippocrates, wan and drawn, exhibiting all the 'hippocratic' symptoms associated with dying. Apparently in my dream handsome Esculapus is trying to repress his fellow Hippocrates but only half succeeding. Thus the aspirate of the repressed image becomes appended to his own name giving the otherwise reassuring context a somewhat threatening undertone.)

*

We are always surprised when reading nineteenth-century translations to find that words now current in our vocabulary are here translated. In a Conan Doyle I find mention of 'vachers' galloping through the American Far West and it takes me quite some time to realise what it's all about, since the word 'vachers', though correct, doesn't fit into the picture. Similarly the London 'cafés' occurring in another passage instead of the expected 'pubs' seem totally out of place. This is because a foreign word, once it is established, retains its original familiarity, whereas the evicted French word has become exotic and strange, almost foreign and definitely unfamiliar.

*

Triteness of the novel.—Triteness is the genre's

congenital weakness from which only the wariest
novelist who takes all the necessary precautions, can
hope to safeguard himself. Because it does not develop
as such things do in real life. It proceeds directly from a
constitutional flaw which leaves the novelist at the
mercy of gross romanticism in a sphere which is
inaccessible to reason or to artistic rigour.

As we all know, the novelist enjoys unparalleled
freedom in the choice and handling of his subject. He
can say what he likes, as he likes and make up his story
according to the whims he claims as his most sacred
right. He invents his characters and deals with them as
he pleases. And what is more, he doesn't even bother
to say where they come from or from whence he
observes them, what has led him to choose his vantage
point if he has one, and why, having chosen it he
doesn't stick to it but wanders at random in every
possible spatial and temporal direction. Where is the
narrator when he sees all the things he describes?
Inside one character and thus outside all the others, or
inside all those whose thoughts and feelings he reports?
What can he reasonably observe from his self-
appointed vantage point? If he occupies a definite
position in relation to his characters, why does he
sometimes know nothing of their motives and at others
know their most intimate thoughts even before they
have thought them? The vantage point problem leaves
the literary world more or less indifferent. Though the

aesthetic level of a story depends largely on how it is solved it is of little interest to novelists apart from the few outstanding exceptions—James, Flaubert, Kafka —who have raised the novel above its inherent vulgarity, while critics usually seem unaware of its very existence and literary historians never have much time for it—or at least don't let it influence their appreciation, especially when they are dealing with big-wigs (indeed who would quibble with a Balzac or a Tolstoy over the inconsistency of a vantage point and the consequent sloppiness of the narrative?). Though by and large novelists are only too ready to talk about the 'treasures' and 'truths' their books contain they have not the slightest inclination to discuss the one aspect of their work on which the critic may legitimately hope to be enlightened. This is obvious from introductions where authors state their intentions—more perhaps to protect themselves against censure than to benefit their readers. They expatiate on the universal significance of their works as mediators of ideas and promoters of progress. Some pride themselves on being informative, educational and even elevating, while others, especially of late, assert that they write novels in order to challenge or condemn the genre. But few if any expect to be judged exclusively according to the rightness and rigour of their methods, though these are the only controllable aspects of their reality.

This is where the modern novel departs from the original form created by a Cervantes or a Defoe. For these novelists who were still under the influence of the epic genre and very much aware of the inevitable arbitrariness of their own, the main thing was to avoid the accusation of extravagance and vulgarity levelled at this *unorganised* genre by writers who were accustomed to identify art with order. Thus if the novelty they heralded was to be accepted they could not resort to the discretionary powers of invention, since invention was precisely what was most suspect. Indeed, if their works were to be appreciated they must not be presented as inventions but as something which had been communicated to them by an exterior agent together with the right or even the obligation to publish it. The convention was not, as some would have it, a legacy from the past, but a means of legitimising and establishing something entirely new. Everybody is familiar with the expedients used by the classical novelist to prove he isn't making things up— the manuscript discovered by chance, the eye-witness account, the confession, old letters unearthed, descriptions of true incidents or adventures—all equally valid so long as they create the illusion of an unknown author for whom the real one only acts as proxy. Such writers, far from presenting their works as the product of original inspiration or the expression of their inner selves, did all they could to shelve the responsibility.

Cervantes, if we take his word for it, had no hand in the creation of *Don Quixote*. All he did was to translate into Castilian the manuscript of a certain Cid Hamet Ben Engeli found by chance in a junk shop. And Daniel Defoe repeatedly asserts that *Robinson Crusoe* is no product of his imagination but an account of real adventures which he has simply written down without changing the sequence or significance of events in any way. Because novelists at the beginning of the modern era preferred to be taken for imitators, translators or compilers rather than to be classed among the common inventors and story-tellers which the term 'novel' evoked, and in order to persuade the reader that they had nothing in common with such a rightly despised, shifty breed, they resorted to any device, however improbable, which might even briefly ward off the accusation of story-telling.

The convention on which the early novel was based, besides dissociating its author from a discredited genre, presented the further advantage of automatically maintaining him within the single vantage point from which his characters were first *perceived*—he could and must know nothing more than what the manuscript, confession, letters or eye-witness could reveal. Since the imaginary agent usually spoke in the name of an 'I' or a 'he' who was central to the action, the real author too was obliged to confine himself to this exclusive account, generally more enlightening as to the character's actions than his psychological motivations. Thus so long as the novel maintained the conventions which purported to exclude it from the genre, it obviously had to forego the more ambitious aims of later, increasingly sophisticated forms. And though such conventions were doubtless restrictive, they did ensure the internal consistency and aesthetic unity which constitute an indispensable criterion of excellence for the evaluation of contemporary literature.

When the nineteenth-century novelist set out to conquer unexplored regions of reality and thought, he was evidently at odds with traditional principles of unity which would thwart his need for absolute freedom. Once the narrator had ceased to acknowledge the limitations of sensory perception, he had to break the artistic rule bequeathed by his forebears. For if he presumed to see and understand everything and to reproduce it faithfully, if he wanted to control both reality and thought, he must obviously lay claim to theoretically unlimited powers of perception and to the superhuman gift of temporal and spatial ubiquity. The classical novelist—who had on the whole only two forms of expression, the narrative and the dramatic or dialogue form—adjusted his method to the fact that he was a single individual, an ordinary human being with the ordinary human being's limited perceptions. He didn't describe or relate anything which a normal person standing beside him couldn't have heard or seen. And he only judged events and people within a context which logically entitled him to do so (the tale might be fanciful and fantastic, yet he still had to conform to the laws of space and time governing all human messages: Gulliver may well be transported to another world with other rules and motives, he knows of his surroundings no more than what he is told and he sees and hears no more than any man, suddenly landed in Brobdingnag or Lilliput, might see and hear).

The new novelist could obviously not conform to this unwritten law which required that his stories, however uninhibited by empirical experience they might be, had nonetheless to submit to intellectual and psychological norms. For him the novel could perceive and express everything. Neither physical limitations nor the opacity of soul and mind could restrain it. Thus the novelist's tale can no longer consist of the alternating dialogue and description which maintained his forebears on a narrowly circumscribed stage where only what can be perceived from a given point of view is represented. He requires new methods to conquer the world of his dreams, other more flexible conventions that will enable him to overthrow old laws. So he invents ingenious contraptions which allow him to hover, weightless in a misty nowhere. And while the frontiers of his empire spread, in a

century that might well be called his own, he
insinuates himself with increasing ease between
related facts and spoken words, between the obvious
and the imaginary, between the body's outer hide and
the inner flesh of the living. In the end there is nothing
his claim to universal knowledge doesn't encompass.
Free from the restrictions which maintained his
predecessors within the compass of physics and logic,
he can take apart the mechanisms of the human soul as
well as those of world history and set himself up, not
any longer as a simple reporter of supposedly true or
possible events, but as an inspired prophet, a seer to
whom life spontaneously reveals both its trivial
quotidian mysteries and the enigmas of its vast
upheavals.

In his famous review of Mauriac's *la Fin de la nuit*,
Sartre discusses the relation between a novel's
shallowness and its author's megalomania. Admittedly
Sartre's outlook is philosophical and he is mainly
concerned with Mauriac's manipulation of his
heroine. But he observes nonetheless that the story's
mediocrity—all the more disturbing in such a high-
minded novel—is a consequence of the author's
unnatural omniscience. To treat a character as Mauriac
treats Thérèse Desqueyroux, says Sartre, is to make a
bit too free with the divine attributes of ubiquity,
omniscience and omnipotence. Moreover it totally
deprives the protagonists of all freedom since the

author, who knows more about their inner thoughts than anybody and sometimes even themselves can know, has determined their line of action from the start. For Sartre the philosopher, the novelist's unforgivable sin—pride, as he rightly calls it—consists in confining his characters to such bondage, and the absence of artistry is no more than an inevitable consequence ('God is not an artist and neither is M. Mauriac.'). Obviously there is a relation between a novel's lack of distinction and the more or less explicit ideology inherent in the need to romanticise. But if the novelist wants to avoid this twofold sin against art and humility, a more honest and healthy attitude of mind is not entirely sufficient. He must also resort to a stricter technical discipline precisely when his megalomania is most imperative. Thus it is incorrect to say that 'M. Mauriac is not a novelist.' He is as much a novelist as any story teller who doesn't react against the form's lack of rigour, or at least acknowledge and be wary of it.

Theoretically it seems that the only way to raise the novel above mediocrity would be to write anti-novels and to subdue its anarchic, conflicting and mostly irrational tendencies by adequate technical means. And theoretically this may be so. But in a sphere where arbitrariness is the rule theory is often disproved by fact, as any one will admit after a cursory glance at the world's masterpieces. Indeed there are few novelists, even among nineteenth or twentieth-century masters, who are not at least to some extent the disciples of that limping demon famed for his ability to lift up the roofs of houses and discover all that goes on beneath and that would be better ignored. The case of Dostoevsky (wrongly—for once—quoted by Sartre as a model Mauriac should try to live up to) is an example among many of the demon's ability (whether he be lame or otherwise) to dispense with logic. Although in his short stories Dostoevsky maintains the classical writer's vantage point outside fictional events, his great novels are, in this respect, most inconsistent. Thus *The Devils* is first narrated by an 'I' who asserts that he was present when everything happened and who, since he has even played a minor part in these events, sometimes lapses into the plural 'we'. Up to a given point in the novel this 'I' has no advantage over any other living 'I'—some facts are known to him, some are not, some he knows by hearsay and some he deduces or reconstructs from facts or fragments of information—but he never oversteps the limits of human intelligence and perception, and his story develops within such limits of which, moreover, he seems to be exceptionally aware —when presenting facts he is wary, reticent and full of reservations; when in doubt he stresses his perplexity and frequently provides alternative versions of an event so that the reader can decide which is most plausible. By using formulae such as 'I heard say . . . ', 'someone maintains that . . . ' etc., he gives the impression of being caught in a tangle of causes and effects of which he is no better judge than anybody else would be in similar circumstances. He does his best to gather the scattered strands of the story around characters who are no more enlightened than he is as regards their own fate, and thus he proves by his very presence that the 'devils' are not motivated by the author's volition but by individual and collective powers unwittingly set in motion by the devil each one bears within himself.

The psychological vagueness which is typical of Dostoevsky's style and whose absence from Mauriac's novel Sartre deplores, is consistently maintained up to this point through the use of a suitable vantage point. But suddenly the 'I' who tells the story vanishes. He has apparently become redundant since what takes place henceforth is common knowledge and can therefore be reported without his assistance. The scrupulous narrator is now ousted by the author who doesn't have to justify his vantage point since he inhabits a non-place where neither outer perception nor inner revelation are denied him.

Most critics who mention this strange transition from 'I' to 'he' see it as proof of carelessness. Yet how then can they account for the fact that the author commits an identical blunder in another novel? For in

The Brothers Karamazov the story is also told by two narrators—the first coming from the same 'district' as the hero and thus acquainted by hearsay with all the intricacies of the tragedy, and the other—who takes over in the fourth chapter—an infallible visionary rather than a common eye-witness. The first reports the whole affair with the caution and reticence of an ordinary witness, while the other who has evidently been granted omniscience by some unknown deity, describes everything in the minutest detail. But in this case carelessness can hardly be invoked to account for the story's flagrant inconsistency since the scrupulous 'I' of the first section never completely disappears but intermittently introduces some uncertainty into the unqualified assertions of the transcending 'he', as if the author vaguely recalled his original plan only to dismiss it in favour of his personal deification.

Though the case of Dostoevsky is particularly conclusive he is by no means the only writer to sacrifice the story's logic and unity to his instinctive megalomania. In the Grand Century of the novel most of the writers to whom the genre owes its extraordinary success succumbed to some extent at least to the heady satisfaction of possessing divine power over their characters. And with the exception of a few who felt that gross romanticism had to be governed by the epic rule which alone could curb it, no one seems to have been aware of the serious aesthetic damage their works suffered in consequence.

Balzac—an all-seeing, prolific novelist if ever there was one—is quite remarkably uninhibited in this respect. He circulates freely in the extensive world of his novels where he selects the spot from which either anything or practically nothing is revealed to him, so that alternately omniscient and almost entirely ignorant, he can float above a population which instantly responds to his magic wand (or to the famous walking stick inscribed with the presumptuous motto on which Kafka wistfully commented: 'On Balzac's walking stick: I shatter every obstacle; on mine: every obstacle shatters me.'). Here we have him in a Paris street by night, walking behind an unknown passer-by. Who is this man? What is he doing? Where is he going? Why does he cast such suspicious glances around as he crosses this lonely bridge? The narrator knows nothing. The passer-by is a perfect stranger who suddenly emerged from the darkness. He only followed him because what little he saw suggested some kind of mystery. Well and good. So we expect him to go on shadowing this man until he reaches his destination and probably disappears from sight. But not at all. The man enters a house and the narrator, instead of staying outside as logic would have it, accompanies him into a crowded room and is promptly transformed from an ordinary onlooker into an invisible, insubstantial familiar, gifted into the bargain with second-sight. One minute the stroller was a faceless, nameless stranger to him, and the next he knows him down to his Balzacian character's core, so that he is able to tell us who he is, why he was out in the night behaving so oddly and furthermore all sorts of minor biographical details and even genealogical accidents—indeed things nobody could possibly know about anyone except he who has made him up. Once again the eye-witness acting as 'I' before the reader is evicted from the story by a ubiquitious, all-knowing 'he'. And here too careless-ness or oversight disguise the author's desire for total control, even at the cost of verisimilitude.

The novel's aesthetic shallowness is mainly due to such paradoxical relations to reality, which lead the whole genre further and further from what traditional story-tellers had ever imagined or hoped. Whereas the classically defined story borrowed from *literature* the technical norms which would ensure its *form*, the more recent novelist tries to extract from *existence* the living *force* they want to set in motion: force and not form is their real aim, and they don't care whether or not their art suffers in the process, since what matters to them now is not to achieve something that conforms to a prescribed model but only the amount of energy directly extracted from nature and society which they are confident of being able to reproduce. In such circumstances it is easy to see why, when Tolstoy

decided to write *War and Peace*, he would have no truck
with conventions that had guided a Swift or a Defoe in
the composition of their works. As absolute master of
his fiction before which History itself must make way,
he had to know what was going on in every mind, on
every stage and wherever his vast population of
characters was scattered. He had to be everywhere at
once or stay in one place without having to justify the
discrepancies between various sections of his novel.
He had to be able to dwell for as long as he pleased on a
trivial household incident or pass over twenty years of
his hero's life in a couple of lines, to leave the room
where he had lingered, apparently for his own
delectation, to describe a little girl being dressed, and
dash off to the battle of Borodino. He had to know
exactly what Lavrouchka, the Cossack, was thinking
during his interview with Napoleon, what he said and
what he didn't say, what the Emperor replied, at what
precise moment the interpreter smiled and why
Thiers, who reported the incident on the basis of his
meagre historical knowledge, provided such a biased
and completely mistaken version. Novelists can indulge such whims without incurring the slightest
blame. It is their right, and the more forceful they are
(in the age of the novel force is everything) the less
scrupulous they have to be in asserting their exceptional, literally unlimited powers. To this they are
entitled—or rather they have the supreme ability to

make everybody believe that they are entitled to it. And in the light of this ability which gives them immense authority over their contemporaries and an impregnable position in the history of ideas, their worst defects appear so insignificant that they do not even require forgiveness.

Nonetheless when Thomas Mann writes: 'Hush, we are about to peer into someone's soul!' or Balzac: 'She had the lightness of step characteristic of all young Parisian women between ten and ten-fifteen a.m.'— the vacuity of such remarks (a soul! All young Parisian women at precisely the same hour!) makes the book drop from my hands—after which, admittedly, I pick it up again and continue to read avidly.

*

Books and the times.—Twenty years ago who would have believed that the 'Black Series' detective novel specialising in tales of depravity would one day be sufficiently whitened to become almost edifying! James Hadley Chase's undying hero, that murderer more stupid even than he is ruthless, ever at the mercy of scheming women (at the suggestion of an ardently desired beauty he plots the perfect murder that should ensure both his immunity and the possession of the importunate husband's fortune—were it not for the sudden appearance, after the crime, of the woman's lover for whom she had in fact been keeping herself and the money all along), that vulnerable, irresistibly irresponsible bruiser and prototype of what once epitomised baseness and corruption, is today very nearly rehabilitated by the practically unavoidable sequence of events from which his crimes and his final downfall proceed and which are seen as largely attenuating circumstances. He has graduated from an ordinary blackguard to an Oedipal hero reduced by his frustrated, forbidden desires to a state of semi-bestiality. Though he flounders in his murky Inferno he is nonetheless admirable since he is completely dominated by excesses that finally transform him into a figure of tragedy (naturally enough, without involving a literary reassessment of his case).

*

If the prosaic has undergone a sort of rehabilitation—due perhaps to a change in moral standards—the poetic, on the other hand seems to me to have suffered a notable deterioration insofar as it aims at broad generalisations and striking ideological contrasts. When I read one of Novalis' many aphorisms where the ontological verb 'to be' is used to make sweeping assessments of value—for instance: 'The breast is the bosom raised to the status of mystery' (there are many others in this vein since analogy here becomes method) —such vagueness parading as truth jars on my intellectual nerves, and I begin to wonder why I ever admired him. What has happened is that in the meantime Kafka has cut the German Romantics down to size, first in Germany by extolling Kleist's incomparable prose which really puts the complacency of their own to shame, and then abroad by forcing us to measure all our grand approximations against the strictures he imposes on himself.

*

Lenin in Zurich. Or is it perhaps Solzhenitsyn himself who is getting ready to leave Zurich on October the 17th to go and assume power in Russia? Snugly installed in Lenin's body and mind the biographer is naturally aware of all that goes on inside him at every moment of the day and of the night. He is quite at home and oblivious of the fact that he may be trespassing or that such complete identification with a historical character—and what a character!—might be considered irresponsible. He is assured that he possesses an intimate knowledge of his hero's unspoken thoughts—those of which he was conscious as well as the unconscious ones that no stenographer in the world could have transcribed—of his throbbing headaches, the cold that penetrates his very bones, his

passing indispositions and even of the painful symptoms of his illness. He knows all and relates all with an
unsuspecting indiscretion (or half-conscious bitchi-
ness) worthy of a great nineteenth-century novelist.
Since he has an unswerving faith in the power of his
vision and the importance of his mission he can create
the illusion that the portrait he is able to evoke is
drawn from life. And the worst of it is that he
succeeds by such wholly indefensible means—here for
once history and literature agree—to infuse into his
Lenin in Zurich so much exuberant vitality that we
tend to be taken in without ceasing to be conscious of
the fraudulence of such romantic licence (the reader
who objected—in a letter to *le Monde*—to the 'bad
language' Solzhenitsyn ascribes to his hero misses the
point altogether. The author is not interested in the
faithfulness of his account. He fashions his man from
the material of his choice and after the model he
fancies. That's all there is to it.).

*

The present is obscure and we make matters worse by
trying to convince ourselves that it isn't. Not that the
present misleads us—to be obscure and appear trans-
parent isn't one of its peculiarities but corresponds
rather to some quirk of our nature whereby we live in
the past and believe we are keeping step with the

times. Actuality, like the theologians' god, is always hidden and we can only persuade ourselves of the contrary by overlaying its opacity with words (in this respect communication inevitably destroys actuality since even the most recent event is assessed when it is communicated and thus becomes part of our intellectual baggage).

*

The rules that govern the transliteration of literary works are either too whimsical to be comprehensible or simply do not exist, and transliteration is a matter of pure chance. Authors whom one would have expected to be practically unexportable because of the pronounced foreign accents they preserve even in the best translations, or because they owe their distinction to highly localised living and creative conditions, cross frontiers without the slightest difficulty and are successfully integrated into the outside world—sometimes as soon as they have been recognised at home, sometimes long after and sometimes long before. (Such was the case with Kafka who, admittedly was nowhere at home and was only famous *elsewhere*, notwithstanding the prediction of Franz Werfel— another native of Prague—who said that 'no one would ever understand Kafka beyond Tetchen-Bodenbach'. Though Kafka's immaculate style obviously makes the apparent oddities derived from his peculiar background much more acceptable.) Other authors from whose writings the total absence of local colour or over-subtle idiomatic expressions would seem to make them generally acceptable are indefinitely excluded from universal libraries and ignored even by their next-door neighbours. For instance, why has Lichtenberg never become popular in France where, over the past two centuries German philosophy has intermittently invaded French culture causing untold havoc? Apart from his concise, incisive style which radiates intelligence and logical lucidity and should have appealed to the French taste, Lichtenberg presents the further advantage of having remained after two centuries, surprisingly undated, notably for his conflicting intellectual make-up which fluctuates between strict rationalism and morbid sensitivity. The inventor of the famous 'bladeless knife without a handle' was more than just the black humorist celebrated by André Breton in his anthology. He was a writer wholly dedicated to the spirit of literature who dreamt up an oeuvre he never wrote except for the wilfully truncated fragments represented by his *Aphorisms*. He was a free thinker whose authentic knowledge of science and especially of suffering safeguarded him against the national, social and racial prejudices held by his reputedly most open-minded successors (Hegel!). And he was a dreamer who dreamt neither of Novalis' Blue Flower nor of Jean-Paul's Lost Paradise, but like Freud exactly a century later, of those inner depths and spaces which the luminaries of his age had neither the means, the inclination nor the courage to explore. Why, notwithstanding all the efforts expended to introduce him, do we continue to ignore this profound and lucid thinker, simultaneously melancholy and lighthearted, gifted with an insatiable curiosity for all that concerns language, yet entirely innocent of those crimes against language of which so many German philosophers are guilty? Why is this intelligent poet condemned to remain on the threshold of our cultural world? Is it precisely because of his lucidity, because his aphorisms ignore clichés, or because he belongs to an out-moded age? I don't know. Moreover I only quote him as an example—a disturbing example, perhaps, if we consider that even in well-informed circles one of the most brilliant names of German literature is frequently confused over here with André Lichten-berger, indisputably one of the dreariest of our writers.

*

Further thoughts on the obscurity of the times.— Nothing shows up the limitations of the imagination better than science fiction.

Anyone who still believes in the Romantic notion of the imagination should be promptly dissuaded by the perusal of these highly unrealistic stories whose sole aim is to evoke the horrors of a future age. For if they prove anything at all it is precisely that however hard we try we can only imagine what is 'past'—with variations, of course, to give our psychic ultra-conservatism an air of independence. Try as it may to anticipate the future by a complacent show of technical devices (which are not even inventions but only deductions from what is already there) science fiction's fundamental regressiveness emerges from its favourite themes. It delves into the backwaters of time to re-enact *ad nauseam* the ancient myths of which our imagination is never tired (that is the secret of its attraction) and its predicaments are not so much about terrors to come as about primal ancestral dreads, about the fascination of the abyss where the first Titans dwelt, the fear of Chaos and the yearning for the uncreated. Notwithstanding its claim to realism its gadget-armoured monsters and unidentified fauna are unmistakably descendants of the fabulous dragons whose prodigious power capable of wiping out creation, whose heroic opponents and bloodthirsty confrontations, existed long before the dawn of historical time. Were it not for the genre's peculiar jargon Hercules would have no difficulty in recognising his Hydra, Oedipus his Sphinx, Siegfried the

Dragon whose blood renders invulnerable those upon whom it falls and the fairy-tale hero the foul monster he has to slay in order to acquire fame. Don Quixote would probably find these new romances of chivalry linguistically very inferior to his own, but he would certainly be delighted to re-encounter his chimeras and andryargues, albeit in a rather unpleasant disguise, and would moreover congratulate himself for this unmitigated confirmation of the great law he untiringly proclaimed: our elementary psychic grammar allows us to talk in the present tense, constrains us unconsciously to think in the preterite, but makes no provision for the future whose conjugation is necessarily modelled on the past.

*

Television programme: *Reading Madame Bovary.*— Pierre Dumayet had asked three inhabitants of a Bourguignon village to read and discuss the novel. They had been invited to select the passage they found most appealing or interesting and to discuss the reasons for their choice. These people represented three distinct aspects of rural life and, apart from living in the same village, seemed to have little in common. One—an elderly peasant woman whom I first took for a man because of her voice and the way she was dressed—trudged along behind her plough and seemed to be both amused and bored by the questions she was required to answer (perhaps she felt that this unusual distraction from her daily tasks was an unwelcome waste of time). Then came a young woman farmer, rather too un-countrified for her part—though once she was settled in her cow-shed she was quite at ease milking the cows. She was extremely articulate and spoke with what should have been a Bourguignon accent but to me had something vaguely Russian. And lastly a M. de Rambuteau introduced as the great-grandson of Napoleon's chamberlain—though I saw him as first cousin to the Count de Faverges or even his spiritual brother, notwithstanding the century's time-lag. Until Pierre Dumayet's intrusion into their lives none of them seemed to have ever heard of Emma Bovary's adventures, except perhaps for the Squire— though even after being shown his well-stocked family library I have my doubts. The old peasant woman was obviously surprised to have found that her professional interest had been aroused by the account in a certain passage of the expert use of a harness breech-band. By and large her sympathies were entirely for Emma whom she found more to be pitied than blamed. Emma was young and beautiful, Charles was stupid and boring, while Leon was both handsome and agreeable, so how could Emma help falling in love with him? It was only natural, not to say inevitable. The young woman farmer was more reserved. On the whole she was reticent and rather uncommunicative, answering in monosyllables as though she were afraid to let herself go on such a risky subject. How come, asked Dumayet relentlessly, that after finding so much to say about the first part of the novel she had no comments to make once Rudolph had arrived on the scene? She didn't know. She had no idea. But when pressed she finally admitted—or at least he dragged the admission from her—that she found the whole incident most unsavoury on account of Rudolph, precisely, whom she considered contemptible. And why? Because he was heartless and base, since while apparently in love with Emma he was already thinking of the best way to be rid of her once she would have ceased to attract him.

As to the Squire he was obviously not interested in the love story, but his description of Humais as 'fundamentally and intrinsically anti-clerical' was certainly heart-felt. As was his observation that, unfortunately, this despicable breed was still thriving, whatever people might say to the contrary. Curiously enough he was the only one to take advantage of the situation to express his opinions. The two women had only feelings and morals.

This little psycho-drama unwinding to a rhythm dictated by the medium and on a friendly, even key, was obviously not likely to provoke a passionate response. Nor was that its purpose. It was intended to amuse and surprise or perhaps embarrass the audience and thus, thanks to a tactful producer, make its point without over-stressing it. But in all this, where was Flaubert? And where was literature? Nowhere, apparently. How could either have a place in such an alien environment where the intervention of language between reality and dream was redundant to the extent of being more trouble than it was worth?

*

Further thoughts on what the Germans call the 'Rezeption' of foreign works (they tend to 'receive' a great deal, whence the need for this special branch of research).—Among the writers who have remained practically unknown outside their own country notwithstanding their apparent accessibility, the most unlucky was probably the Alemanite poet Robert Walser. True this inveterate vagabond and inspired novelist of the art of failure tried harder than anyone else to stay in the background and, indeed, passed practically unnoticed across the literary scene. Robert Walser—who was incapable of submitting to any kind of discipline and who, to make doubly sure of not succeeding, spent thirty years of his life in a mad-house without even writing his 'Ode to Folly'—persisted in being if not by any means a run-of-the-mill failure, at least the perfect misfit, the champion of nothingness and a volunteer for obscurity. But, although even in this respect he was not entirely successful, since in Germany a handful of enthusiastic admirers see him as the great poet he was, he did defy the laws of success to the extent of maintaining abroad the kind of literary non-existence he strove for. (Even Kafka's partial debt to him has not been recognised and my translations of his masterpiece, *Jakob von Günten*, and of the odd bits of prose I published in periodicals, have passed unnoticed except by a few readers capable of perceiving the bleeding heart his reticence so successfully disguises—they received barely three pages of criticism followed by the inevitable silence!)

Apart from what it owes to his own particularity Walser's non-existence abroad may well be due to the common phenomenon that a book written and published without the support of an author, a publisher or some dedicated group, may perhaps be acknowledged in its own country but never beyond its frontiers where a nobody remains a nobody unless a friend, a disciple or a translator takes the case to heart. (If Kafka's instructions had not been ignored by Max Brod his fate would have been similar to Walser's. He and his writings would have known the oblivion to which he basically aspired.)

Of course Walser's case is exceptional. A writer is usually unpopular abroad for less personal reasons such as chauvinism, for instance, which accounts for the rejection of a number of foreign authors in France during certain periods. Why isn't Theodore Fontane, that typical late nineteenth-century German novelist, recognised in this country when Russia and Scandinavia have opened their doors to him? The significance of his work and his local fame should have entitled him to such recognition. But unfortunately he was misguided enough to be born a Prussian, to delight in depicting his native Brandenburg countryside and to be inordinately fond of Berlin. Moreover when posted to France as war correspondent in 1870 he was arrested for espionage, which could hardly endear him to my countrymen. However, although Prussia has been wiped off the map and can no longer be the object of our hatred, the banishment which affected Fontane during his life has not been abrogated and, as far as I know, the works of this remarkable Brandenburg Flaubert have never been translated into French.

*

Art and Essay.—While Rosa Luxembourg was compiling her great treatise on political economy she wrote to a friend—from prison I believe—that she would not be satisfied till she had succeeded in giving to this exceptionally difficult work the formal perfection of a poem. Not that she had any intention of mitigating the aridity of her subject by stylistic effects.

But she was convinced that unless she could adapt her literary efforts to her ends and create for each section the form and mood required by the content, she would have failed to convey the truth even of those theories to which she was most profoundly dedicated. As a result her work was never accessible to the lay reader and is said to be so impenetrable that barely a couple of specialised Marxist scholars have ever been able to fully appreciate it.

*

As a rule I am prepared to like anyone whom those I consider most worthy of respect admire (with the momentous exception of Goethe, whose enormous influence on so many totally unbiased minds is to me completely incomprehensible—here, for some inexplicable reason, I cannot follow). When my personal motives for admiring someone are already strong enough to require no further confirmation, I still feel that they acquire an extra dimension when they have passed along this unbroken chain of admiration, this sort of spiritual inheritance. Confronted with Flaubert's unwavering passion for Cervantes, Georg Büchner's extraordinary memorial to Lenz which sets this unhappy poet's tattered life in true perspective, Brecht's translations of Villon and Baudelaire's of Poe or Kafka's vision of Strindberg as a gigantic statue clasping him to its heart as one would a frightened child, I feel that something emerges from the depths of time which is not just another chapter in the history of literature but literature itself, the essence of literature which would probably still be unidentified were it not for this intense traffic of thoughts and feelings maintained in perpetual motion by our masters.

*

Though it is undoubtedly exhilarating to find that a writer admires an ancient or modern text we consider admirable, it is most disturbing to discover that something we had always taken for a personal fad is also shared. For instance there is a passage in Judges— almost unbelievably modern in the cynicism with which incredible atrocities are reported—which has always fascinated me. It is the account of what happens to the Levite of Mount Ephraim during his sojourn among the Benjamites. When a band of Sodomites peremptorily invite him to come out of the house where he has been given shelter for the night, he calmly hands over his concubine and goes back to bed where he sleeps peacefully till day-break when, as he sets forth to pursue his journey, he finds the woman's dead body on the threshold. Without a word he slings it over his ass's saddle and rides home. On his arrival he divides the corpse 'together with the bones' into

twelve portions which he sends to the twelve tribes of
Israel. Why is such a tale included in the Holy Text?
What can one make of it over and above what the facts
clearly state? Why has it been practically canonised? It
contains no apparent symbolic message, invokes neither
pity, indignation nor an elementary sense of justice. It
has no moral unless it be that it is better to rape a
woman than violate the laws of hospitality. Moreover,
though it is a memorable incident, the Levite of Mount
Ephraim unlike most biblical characters, has not been
glorified either by posterity or literature. No one has
ever tried to immortalise his adventures or to unravel
this bloodthirsty mystery. So I had naturally assumed
that I was alone in seeing this story as a little
masterpiece. However I was mistaken. Re-reading the
Confessions more attentively perhaps than hitherto, I
discovered that Rousseau had been similarly struck by
it, that it had engrossed him for a whole night and that
he could only be rid of the obsession by retelling it in
the form of a short story called *The Levite from Ephraim*
which, he declares, remained one of his favourites.
However if Rousseau immortalised the Levite it was
not because of the contrast between the story's
primitive content and the extraordinary modernity of
its form, but because he felt the need to exorcise the
biblical demon—or at least to purify it in the Holy
Waters of his own sensibility.

*

I ought to be very upset at the vast number of books to be read which I haven't read, but I'm not because, as far as some of them are concerned, it's too late anyway, for others there will always be time, and there are besides a great many I am quite happy to ignore when I think of all those I keep wanting to re-read and which in certain cases I do re-read *ad nauseam*.

*

Great books transform one's life, good books brighten it and bad books sadden it because they are bad and there are so many of them, but mainly because there is always a certain point of view from which one sees that one might have written them oneself.

*

All things considered there are only two ways in which novelty can manifest itself in literature. Either tradition is presumed dead and novelty replaces it without more ado. Or traditional themes and methods are mimicked in order to expose, not their immuta-bility, but on the contrary, how artificial and outdated they really are. In the first case novelty can't wait—impatience is its undoing—to proclaim the death-warrant which makes its succession legitimate. Then, on the assumption that its purely verbal proclamation is valid, it behaves—or writes—as if tradition were actually dead and buried. In the second case novelty quietly bides its time. Knowing that tradition has never been deeply affected by the backwash of a stormy avant-garde and has survived many a revolution, it resorts to more sophisticated tactics, feigning submission and fidelity so as to hold up to ridicule traditional mechanisms, stereotypes and basic principles. While affecting unmitigated reverence the better to unmask it, novelty infiltrates the enemy ranks whence it can uncover the secret laws of literary archeology. Never mind if the scout is acclaimed as an original creator or not. What he wants is to uncover the strange coupling of old and new from which all novelty is born, because he knows that so long as he has not exposed the swindle he will continue to be a living proof of the fact that all our calendars are based on time's complicity with timelessness. This is what the novelty of mere propaganda rashly overlooks. Confident that it can do away with tradition by dismissing it—when in fact such overconfidence is precisely what enables tradition to survive—it reduces itself to the status of a late tradition in the inexhaustible academy of the outdated. So that in fact only one form of novelty is possible in literature, and that is *demonstration*, which can take advantage of tradition first by compelling it to self-destruction and then by discovering the secret of its timelessness.

*

Mr Nobody becomes somebody as soon as a contemporary or a spokesman for posterity writes his biography. As the protagonist of a story he is instantly transferred to transcendency where the individual and his adventures become a single apparently pre-ordained entity. In real life he may have lacked all directive, may have drifted with the tide of unfathomable circumstances and left his future biographer nothing but a muddled, discontinuous and almost incomprehensible tissue of events. No matter. As the hero of a structured story he will emerge as the author of a life he probably only endured in the semi-passive semi-blindness common to all human beings. The written account of his life does more than simply rescue him from oblivion. Be it good or bad literature, enthusiastic or guarded, it can't fail to endow him with the faultless integrity of a second death which will make the first clearly meaningful. As the expression of the age-old complicity between the need to write and the need to kill it neatly 'finishes off' its subject.

*

'The interesting' as a category.—In the vocabulary of contemporary criticism this term tends increasingly to exclude all others. Mainly, of course, because it is handy, but also because it helps to promote a proliferation of otherwise undefinable works of literature. Nobody would ever consider using the term when describing a classical work. 'Interesting' obviously only applies to what is and presumably will remain ephemeral. When a work's staying power is an open question it is said to be interesting, thus leaving room for any undetected qualities it might possess while stressing the fact that it has at least the virtue of being the product of our time and so reflects accurately the uncertainty and precariousness of contemporary existence. The interesting has eliminated the beautiful, the true, the accurate and the inaccurate, failure and success from our vocabulary, its one concern being the here and now where we can find confirmation of our own existence and a vindication, if not an actual glorification of its aimlessness. It implies that there is no cause for concern, that today is as good as yesterday, if not better, since it produces nothing which doesn't emanate from our own peculiar essence. But though it tries to make the present bearable by stressing the charm and abundance of its productions —interesting books are as plentiful as true ones are rare—its principal aim, since creative art can't be assessed on the spot, is to do away with assessment altogether and substitute the vague complacency of personal opinion for the precision of considered criticism.

*

Les Cahiers de la Petite Dame.—What first strikes us here is the similarity between the '30s and the present day. Then we gradually realise that such similarity barely disguises the profound distinction which makes any comparison invidious. Admittedly the controversial topics discussed in literary and intellectual circles at the time—Gide's book on the USSR, the Moscow trials, Malraux's involvement or the future of Western civilisation in its apparently losing battle against the powers of destruction—were not unlike today's. But if all this doesn't seem very far removed from our own preoccupations the attitudes and vocabulary are definitely dated. Public figures who felt they had a public part to play discussed universal matters in a personal voice using terms that were never at any time drawn from the abundant store of stereotypes provided by any one of the current ideologies. There were obviously amongst them sympathisers, sceptics, fanatics and the usual contingent of waverers. But people could share the same opinions without necessarily losing their identity. Each one spoke as a private person, naturally motivated by personal likes and dislikes, particular sexual and affective experiences and peculiar faults and qualities, but not by doctrinal discourse. Each one was totally and openly involved and nobody paid too much heed to the disparagement or the insults of formalists who confuse generality and collectivity. Furthermore, in such strictly non-specialised circles controversy was a man-to-man affair even where major contemporary problems were at stake. And since it was based on the radical individualism of an intellectual class which, though profoundly disturbed was no less firmly convinced of its intellectual responsibility (the Little Lady writes that when Gide was asked what he believed to have been the most useful thing he had ever done he replied that he thought it was the part he had played in reducing the proportion of error in the world) it was impossible to foresee who would defend which cause, who would use what argument. (Gide's behaviour in 1940 when Gallimard decided to resume publication of the NRF (Nouvelle Revue Française) is just one example of an intellectual's unpredictability in those days. Gide didn't try to conform to the political or moral code of any party. Rightly or wrongly—sometimes unquestionably wrongly—he acted according to what he felt to be his duty to himself, to his friends and to his ideals.) It is true that the uncommitted writer, unwilling to assume the role of infallible prophet, was already a rear-guard fighter isolated from the main forces. However, as the war and its attendant confusion intervened the conversations reported by the Little Lady gradually change tone. Though the 'I' who speaks is still very sure of his own identity the unmistakably personal and hitherto absolutely unconventional voice shows signs of the fatal weakness which would soon render him defenceless before the onslaughts of the ideology to which he finally conformed.

*

When I read in a newspaper article the sentence: 'Mr. X who is, or thinks he is an atheist . . . ' I am nonplussed. Yet this sort of more or less frankly apologetical assertion is something to which we should have grown accustomed. Admittedly it is usually a little more cautious than here where the writer's bluntness reveals the depths of misunderstanding which surrounds such terms as belief, idea or opinion. Indeed to deny an atheist the right to self-knowledge one must be a more than exceptionally dedicated defender of the Faith—a defender to whom everything is permitted in the furtherance of his cause, even specious arguments and dishonesty. He has moreover to be unaware of the fact since one of the linguistic ambiguities responsible for most misunderstandings, genuine or otherwise, is contained in this assertion.

The first misunderstanding is simple enough. It concerns the verb 'to believe', a most ambiguous verb and one which is put to extensive use for the conversion of reluctant heretics of all persuasions. A believer believes and the verb is no one's business but his own. There is little risk of his competence being challenged or of anyone trying to convince him that he doesn't believe in anything and that his profession of faith stems from a delusion and therefore can't be taken seriously. Of course it's legitimate to challenge faith as such, to deny the reality of its object, to discuss or refute a religious view of the world, but not to question a believer's public declaration since in this respect an act of faith and declaration are one and the same thing. We only have to say 'I believe' to perform an act of faith, to change intention into fact and, unlike subjective beliefs which can't be proved, this fact is as unquestionable as any other spatial and temporal occurrence. When a statesman says 'I declare war' his words are identical with the action which sparks off hostilities. In the same way the word 'credo' instantly performs the conversion which only recantation can cancel. Declarations of war and professions of faith share the ability to create an event in the time it takes to state them. Thus whether justified or not, they are beyond question, no criticism or analysis of what has been asserted will prevent the transition into action implied by the assertive mood. Psychic or historical motives may come to light but no invalidating or discriminatory conclusions can be drawn from them (indeed in the days of faith and inquisitions this was so obvious that the credo, invested with the power to discriminate between true believers and heretics, was an instrument of salvation or perdition).

Although the 'credo's' efficiency has decreased with the gradual secularisation of religion it still works wonders for those who assert a conviction in order to fit themselves into a pigeon-hole. If we declare that we are existentialists, communists or Royalists we may naturally provoke various reactions, be told that our choice is odious, that we don't practise what we preach or that we don't really know what we are doing, but no one will dare remove the tag we have chosen for ourselves nor contest the fact that a choice has been made. It would be absurd to imagine someone writing: 'Mr X. who is or thinks he is a Protestant . . .' because we all know that in such a case a profession of faith reflects a fact which has nothing to do with the scruples, advantages or illusions which might cast some doubt on its significance. However if this linguistic law is generally respected as something that makes individual behaviour plausible, atheists are systematically denied the right to be taken seriously. When they assert that they believe in nothing we remain incredulous, their words carry no weight and appear to give no indication of the part they have chosen for themselves. Whereas the believer's word is never questioned though he refers to something which can't be proved, that of the atheist and the sceptic is suspect by definition and the more unambiguously it is asserted the more suspiciously will it be received. This is how faith fakes its revenge on non-faith—it proclaims that the disbeliever doesn't know what he says or does and only believes that he doesn't believe in anything, thus leaving him at the tender mercies of the verb 'to believe' from which precisely he would assert his independence.

One of the nicest examples of such scepticism concerning a sceptic alive or dead (the dead are obviously its ideal victims) is the attitude of some of Freud's interpreters towards a man whose writings would seem to be a most unlikely target. It is a well-known fact—and one that he himself asserted at various stages of his life—that Freud was both theoretically and practically a staunch agnostic. Indeed, from quite early on he had come to regard agnosticism as an essential condition of sanity. He believed in none of the things religion and philosophy preach and, unlike so many others whose loss of faith is accompanied by remorse and scruples, he seemed to be so utterly serene one can but assume he felt neither. One would have thought that so unwavering a man, whose ideas were so unambiguously expressed, might discourage any of those attempts at posthumous conversion to which famous rebels are so often sub-jected. But in fact his assertions on the subject are dismissed and the Discoverer of the Unconscious has even been represented in writing as a true mystic disguised as a disbeliever for personal reasons or in order to placate the scientific world of his day. This, apparently, is vindicated by the fact that he was interested in dreams, in the secrets of the soul and in superstitions—his own, which he couldn't discard, as much as those of the patients he analysed—in fact in all the disturbing phenomena through which divinity terrifyingly reveals itself to man. Even Freud's ex-plicit rejection of such an interpretation of his scien-tific preoccupations is seen as an added proof of his stubborn refusal to see himself as he really was.

Naturally enough apologists can provide no detailed evidence for a faith that fits so uneasily into our image of Freud. First because they would be hard put to do so, and secondly because any 'credo' however vague and insignificant, is better than none. Moreover such an activity isn't really designed to bring lost sheep back to the fold but rather, through Freud, to undermine a general tendency towards intellectual secularisation, of which he was indeed an inspired pioneer. Because, obviously, if the major opponent of religious illusions was an unconscious believer, or rather if he believed against his will and against his dearest theories, then everybody must have some kind of religious faith, there is no point in distinguishing one opinion from another, and the so-called history of ideas is a redundant myth.

*

The meaning acquired in current usage by the word 'confrontation' gives food for thought. It is naturally a weak word. Borrowed from the vocabulary of juris-diction and disputation it is quite inadequate for the role assigned to it in private arguments or public declarations. Why has such an insignificant word been chosen, rather than so many others which would have served just as well to express so momentous a split between one individual and the rest of society? Maybe on account of its weakness, which would make it seem exceptionally apt to describe the intended ambiguity? Or was it chosen perhaps for its inability to turn an ordinary squabble into a serious conflict? Or again because the contrast between its original and its acquired meaning created the right sort of inde-terminacy? However that may be the term's popu-larity has not made it any more forceful. In fact it has become so puny in the last decade or so that the 'confronter' unlike the subversive or the rebel, can hardly expect to be recorded other than fleetingly by historians of his time.

*

Why are certain clearly defined words whose mis-appropriation is due to a considerable degree of ignorance so popular with lecturers and writers today? 'Avatar' for instance, infallibly misinterpreted as a synonym for mishap, injury, accident or what-have-you, is pronounced and written with a relish hardly to be accounted for by its relative uncommonness. Even generally discriminating writers can't resist it. Apparently the pleasure obtained from pointlessly miscon-struing a word, often more or less unwittingly, weighs more in the balance than the fear of making a fool of oneself and of allowing the undiscovered error to become common property.

*

Dream words are not spelt any old how, though their spelling obviously doesn't obey prescribed rules. Thus the word 'holopenthes' I once dreamt ('Your holo-penthes are going to be taken', said someone to me in a lift which was travelling at nightmare speed sideways rather than up or down), can't be written otherwise than I write it here. Of this I have never had the slightest doubt, despite the objections of those to whom I mentioned the case and who queried such a spelling. Some want to substitute an *a* for the *e* which is

too assertive for their liking. Others find that the two
*h*s constitute a useless refinement, though they can't
decide which one should go. However we finally
settled for my original spelling, especially as I was the
only one who could tell where the word came from.
(Later I understood why my 'holopenthes' would have
been of no use to me with an *a* and only one *h*: the
neologism's prefix associates it directly with 'holo-
caust' and its ending has an obvious relation to
'nepenthes' so that its meaning constitutes a cunning
compromise between the violent death implied by the
notion of sacrifice and the peaceful death resulting
from a magic potion.)

*

According to M. whose assertion is based on extensive
clinical experience, the indicative imperfect is the
tense in which we dream. The others (present or past)
only replace it on false pretence as it were—seemingly
employed to contain the past more effectively, they
actually cancel it out by depriving it of the characteristic indeterminacy of remembered time. When applied
to literature this peculiarity of dream language might
well explain my uncanny aversion to stories of any
kind told in the past or in the present tense. For the
author thus wittingly misleads his readers by giving an
air of finality to reported events which, as such, are

indeterminate and pertain to repetition and suspense. But apart from this irritating juggling with temporality, his rejection of the imperfect tense, whether or not he tries to justify it in theory, is annoying in that, by attempting to abolish the 'once upon a time' which initiates all stories, he is uselessly reacting against an inviolable law of the imagination. (You can't have a 'historical' present in literature. It simply destroys the story. As proof we only have to try writing in the present tense the famous opening sentence of *Bouvard and Pécuchet*: 'Since the temperature was 33° . . .'—or for that matter, any of the famous opening sentences to which all great novels owe their immediate impact.)

*

When I read a phrase such as this one taken at random from *César Biroteau*: . . . 'His thin lips were not without charm; but his pointed nose and slightly bulging forehead suggested a lack of breeding. Moreover his hair—so black it might well have been dyed—revealed the social hybrid whose wits are the legacy of a high-born libertine, whose vulgarity is inherited from a seduced peasant-girl, whose intellect betrays an incomplete education, and whose vices are the result of a neglected childhood . . . ' I am always amazed at the liberties the novelist takes, his disdain for realism and the total implausibility and inanity of

such writing. For Balzac, pointed noses and bulging
foreheads unquestionably denote bastardy (another
character in the story has 'a vulgarly turned-up nose';
evidently a turned-up nose is no better than a pointed
one). And who indeed can question him since his
system of correspondences operates exclusively in his
own subjective world where logic—and even intelligence—are controlled by his will. No ordinary individual, physiognomist or qualified psychologist would
venture to assert that he is fully acquainted with the
relation between a man's face and what lies behind it.
The novelist however has no such compunction. He
knows that appearances only exist to indicate and
signify the inner man. Thus he can translate the man's
nose and forehead into character and class, and
furthermore deduce from the colour of his hair the
origin of his virtues and vices—his wits most certainly
come from the well-born libertine, his vulgarity from
the seduced peasant-girl—and his vices are the consequence of bastardy since those born out of wedlock
must inevitably be dissolute (his tell-tale hair, though
naturally black, gives the impression of being dyed)
and a threat to social stability. Thus if a head of hair is
deemed too dark to be in good taste the well-equipped
novelist can confidently infer the character's inner
disposition complete with basic flaws and dissolute
tendencies. Moreover this same distinctive feature will
enable him to reconstruct a whole drama with untold

social or even cosmic consequences. What more can one ask, even of Balzac who, as the creator of all that constitutes poor Du Tillet, doesn't perhaps require that much insight to obtain such an unusual amount of reliable and delicately varied information from the colour of the fellow's hair? True, the most remarkable feat in such circumstances is precisely to get the reader to overlook this important fact. (Indeed the boundary line might well lie here between the writer of genius whose mind is fertile by definition, and the great rationally-minded writer inhibited precisely by his rationality. Balzac's physio-psychology assumes the stature of a scientific theory before disintegrating into pure inanity. Gogol, on the other hand, who hasn't got a system of correspondences, goes ahead and writes *The Nose* to illustrate his utter bewilderment at having a nose in the middle of his face.)

*

However I am far from suggesting that Balzac is the only novelist to make such indiscriminate use of the art of physiognomy. It is a common practice among most writers who have turned their backs on the epic genre even if they don't usually relate the process to any kind of metaphysics. There is no better way for a novelist to ensure the intense circulation of emotions which has become the novel's main requisite in modern times, than to establish a relation between his characters' appearance and their inscrutable essence. Were it not for the assumption that there exists a direct cause-effect relationship between mind and body which partially betrays the former's secret motivations, how could a novelist create the complex network of feelings and states of mind wherein his characters flounder? How could he evolve from description to intellectual and emotional confrontation? Characters such as Gogol's Tchitchikov who are neither tall nor short, young nor old, handsome nor ugly, whose appearance reveals nothing, belong exclusively to the epic genre. The novel as such, with its pretensions to profundity, would never have any truck with him unless he were first divested of his unobtrusiveness and improved by the addition of a few telling features.

*

Quite by chance I discover a passage in Lermontov indicating that he was much more circumspect than Balzac in his handling of physiognomy. At a given point in his story (*A Hero of Our Time*) Lermontov, struck by the absurdity of what he presumes to have deduced from his hero's expression, questions the validity of such evidence and concludes rather lamely by asserting that we are all entitled to our own personal interpretations. Lermontov had earlier presented his hero from every possible angle describing him, clothes, attitudes, expressions, teeth, hair and all until he comes to the eyes which are always the most revealing features in such portraits. 'When he laughed they (his eyes) didn't laugh . . . a sign either of natural hardness or of profound, unendurable sadness. Under their lowered lashes they shone as though with a phosphorescent glow. But it was a glow which expressed neither passion nor imagination: it was more like the glint of steel, blinding and cold. His quick glance was both piercing and ponderous . . . '. Here the narrator, suddenly aware of the incoherence and implausibility of this description, confesses that he can be sure of nothing and admits that this man might well 'make quite a different impression' on somebody else and that the portrait he has painted represents only what he has seen with his own eyes—which is totally irrelevant since the character is his own invention and can be seen by no one else's. 'But as I am alone in describing him you will have to make do with my description. Let me add that he was rather handsome, having the sort of distinctive good-looks that particularly appeal to women.' Such a wealth of ingenious analysis and subtle psychology to end up with this tritest of clichés! A portrait which started out as a purple passage—it takes two pages—suddenly collapses into comedy. Lermontov has done his duty as a novelist, but the result is that the reader doesn't know what the character ought to look like nor what to make of his looks anyway. At first he will naturally be impressed by the almost painful irony of the conclusion and immensely grateful to the author for his exceptional honesty. But the outburst of sincerity ultimately misfires since the reader will shortly realise that the story's spell has been broken and that his thoughts have wandered to the torments and scruples he rightly ascribes to its author.

*

The change literature has undergone is easier to state than to define. Is it temporary or final? Is it a symptom of death or rebirth? There is certainly something different, but where exactly does the difference reside? In the preoccupations and subject-matter of the works published in the last fifteen years or so—or since much longer perhaps, for modern literature has been restless and rebellious from the start? In the specialised circles where books are produced? In those who write? In the economics of publication? In the relationship of what was once the avant-garde to publishers and the public? Unquestionably in all these, and to such varying degrees that the whole pattern is not easy to define at a glance. But independently from factors having only an extrinsic bearing on literary creation—admitting that such independence is possible—the most significant change apparently concerns the writer's personal attitude to the concept of literature, that is to the convictions, images, hopes and emotions from which literature has always drawn the power to communicate.

Naturally enough the change didn't occur all at once. It was preceded by a number of minor, equally 'modern' upheavals which, in their time were similarly intent on overthrowing, or at least undermining tradition. Romanticism, German Expressionism, Dadaism, Surrealism, all strove for an unlimited freedom involving the dissolution of traditional forms and, as a rule, a more or less total break with the accepted concept of art and creativity. Thus the Surrealists had already advocated spontaneity (to use a term which today applies to all kinds of instinctive manifestations) claiming that art is the prerogative of every dreamer and refusing to conform to conventional notions of creativity. (Someone is said to have predicted that André Breton would be made to pay for his outrageousness by being published in anthologies—which came true, but isn't perhaps such a terrible calamity after all. . . .) Spontaneity is also the most dynamic, or anyhow the most obvious feature of today's 'new' writing (which, unlike previous literary innovations with their manifestoes, labels, founding fathers and disciples, can't or won't answer to a specific denomination). However there exists a notable difference between the two schools, for although André Breton and his followers rejected the idea of 'art' as the product of some mysterious vocation, reorganised classifications and overthrew idols indiscriminately (nobody spared Claudel, and Breton had a personal grudge against Dostoevsky) they did admire all the novelists and poets who corresponded to their ideal—not simply because these were outcasts (all their confederates were not accursed and all the accursed were not on their side), but mainly because, for them creation had been the most unadulterated and earnest of games. In this respect Surrealism didn't try to break with tradition but endeavoured rather to carry it further by strengthening the links between past aspirations and actual rebellions.

I recall Gilbert-Lecomte once saying, 'I judge a man by his capacity for admiration', and every romantic shares this view, even when he doesn't admit it. Surrealist terrorism—which still influences advanced literary attitudes in more ways than one—was largely the consequence of a capacity for admiration which involved the past in contemporary controversies. Admiration tended to be over-zealous. People sided with Rimbaud against Lautréamont, with the 'minor' Romantics against the 'major', with Nerval, Baudelaire and Edgar Allan Poe against Artaud, because he promoted Strindberg. Battles, though frequently fought for the dead, were fierce. Furthermore nobody

was particularly worried by theoretical problems
since what really mattered in such heated confrontations was for each contestant to assert himself and his
views on writing (Roger Gilbert-Lecomte used also to
say 'I consider any man a swine who doesn't write
about main issues'). Reverence for a writer, his status
as model and master, didn't imply that he had been
measured against some ideological yard-stick. It was a
declaration of faith in a given literary ethics, a freely
accepted 'Thou shalt'. It involved primarily constant
familiarity with his works, which were read, quoted,
recited and translated if need be, in order to ritually
ensure a constant flow of emotions and ideas. If you
loved Antonin Artaud you couldn't dissociate him
from Gérard de Nerval (when in 1948 I accompanied
Artaud to a little town in the South of France he spent
his nights reciting Nerval's poems, or rather shouting
them at the top of his voice, which cannot have
allowed our neighbours much sleep during that week).
If you loved Arthur Adamov you had to be prepared to
celebrate with him at all times—such things can't be
postponed—the particular writer living or dead,
famous or obscure, whose unexpectedly discovered
poem, passage or single phrase had just moved him.
His enthusiasm for the art of others, whether Novalis,
Hölderlein, Kleist, Büchner, Gogol, Kafka or Flaubert, was part and parcel of his own art. He positively
thrived on admiration and those who knew him can

vouch for the fact that he was unusually gifted at communicating it. But this extraordinarily communicative enthusiasm obviously had nothing in common with the combination of nostalgia and aggressivity which characterises cultural activity today. It was simply a dedication to literature, because of its capacity to reveal the most basic singularity to as wide a public as possible, and faith in its ability to transmit *realistically* the history of its *imaginary* onslaughts on the boundaries of thought. A book wasn't something to be coveted, nor was it a fetish, in the term's contemporary sense—it simply provided a weapon against life's stagnation, or as Kafka puts it 'the axe that shatters the frozen sea within us.'

Enthusiasm, dedication, message, vision—such words borrowed from the religious vocabulary seem to have no possible connection with the generally atheistic avant-garde. Yet there is no substitute for them here since the literary revolution, while violently rejecting most of the intellectual attitudes inherited from the past century, and especially every form of religious belief, was nonetheless totally uncompromising where its sacred models were concerned. In fact its attitude to literature was pious in proportion to its general sacriligious intentions, so that whether it wanted it or not, a well worn tradition was maintained at least in this context.

As a matter of fact literature has always been

inclined to confer sacred or divine properties upon its technical activities. Writers are inspired, they have vocations or missions and, not infrequently, they are in hell or damned. Literature has its chapels, prophets and ascetics, not to mention the martyrs most biographers reveal (Surrealism even had its 'pope'!). Its aptitude for incantation, invocation and spells relates it to magic, occultism and alchemy and thus provides it with infidels and heretics (whence the successive avant-gardes will recruit its own prophets), and like religion it is entirely based on the absolute authority of Writings which contain both Salvation and the Law.

In the nineteenth century this similarity maintained by current parlance was further corroborated by the sanctification of literature (and of art in general) motivated by a need to compensate for the gradual secularisation of most Western communities. At first the conflation of religious and literary ideals would have served the purpose of the Church—Chateaubriand, Novalis and many others combined them uninhibitedly. But it soon led to misunderstandings for which 'inspired' atheists or simply uncommitted writers were held responsible (thus Rimbaud's desertion of the poetic cause is seen as a betrayal of the mission entrusted to him—an unpardonable sin indeed, unless it can be justified by religious conversion). Towards the close of the century the writer's art, increasingly independent of religious connotations, assumed the role of surrogate faith, tacitly assigned to it by the supreme powers of culture—it was now a 'form of prayer' (Kafka), or as Flaubert perceptively put it: 'the unbeliever's religion.'

In the last fifty years writers have unremittingly attacked the bastions of superstition and piety where self-sanctified literature is peacefully entrenched. Such has generally been the basis from which the new movements took off. For the more far-seeing realised that it was impossible to write with integrity so long as the irrational beliefs, hopes of transcendence and delusions of eternity on which literary vocations thrived, were maintained. Joyce wrote his Odyssey to debunk once and for all the authoritarian and eternal truth of the epic. Brecht claimed that copyright was the major imposture of a frozen culture—an author's works can't be safeguarded, the written text automatically becomes public property and represents a collective, eminently sharable heritage available to all and sundry. Though more restrained, the German Expressionists too attacked the idolisation of works of art which can turn so easily into bigotry and which throws a decorous aesthetic veil over the most shameless social deception. Wherever the foundations of established ideas are being undermined we see literature accused of tacitly—it's the surreptitiousness that's so nauseating—nurturing such survivals from the past as misguided mysticism, messianic hopes and pseudo-spirituality. Obviously literature's self-accusations don't foreshadow its death, but rather the opposite. Since while the age-old irrationality involved in the act of writing is exposed to mockery, satire and parody, it is very far from ignoring the message contained in 'eternal' works which it incorporates into new books aping as it were the enemy in order to stress his incongruity. Solidly anchored to, and buttressed by the past it seeks to discredit, modernity asserts itself *with* its models as much as *against* them, thus acquiring at least some of their charm and a semblance of immortality. So Joyce gets even with Homer in an imposing parody where the epic's generally accepted legitimacy is finally made nul and void. But his Ulysses cannot ignore the *literary* past from which he emerges. He is no less involved with his homonym than with the characters in his story and, while embodying the hero of his day—or of one day—created on purpose to make the hero of all time redundant, what he says in his epoch-making language is nevertheless a reference, a homage and a sort of protracted goodbye to the extinct world of the epic.

Similarly Brecht, who loathes literary sanctity and out-laws himself by asserting the rights of plagiarism, rejects accepted values without however renouncing the models set by literary tradition. He writes with Luther and the brothers Grimm in mind and when asked which book has most influenced him replies:

'You'll laugh: the Bible'. And his writings do not only commemorate the errors and pitfalls of universal literature but also its beauty, wisdom and truth.

As to Kafka I don't think he ever talks about anything but the tragic, absurd and hopeless conflict within him between novelty and tradition—a tradition whose share of truth commands respect, however outdated such a truth may be, and a novelty painfully aware of its precariousness and which represents for him no more than the fragility and charm of transience or, at best the dubious advantage of clear-sightedness. In such circumstances it isn't a matter of innovating by eliminating archaisms, but of confronting the writer with a final choice—to live *normally* so that writing will cease to be a need and become self-glorification, aimless jottings and shameless exhibitionism, or to be *committed* to writing, that is sacrifice his life to the unknown with no possible assurance of satisfaction. We all know how Kafka solved the problem and how in this obviously extreme case scribbling overruled living.

To judge from the rather mixed tendencies expressed by present day movements, modernity seems to have recovered from the passion for literature which yesterday's avant-garde witnessed, suffered and condemned. At any rate there is no sign of it in contemporary literature; writers no longer draw inspiration from the struggle against *and* for tradition.

Indeed it would seem that the latter has been finally silenced and forgotten or is simply not worthy of notice. However, such total scorn for the opposition may well lead to modern literature's downfall. For its very existence depends on the fact that writers once wrote with that peculiar mixture of faith, doubt and innocence which somehow does seem to modify reality. What, after all, is literature if not a legend, a system of fictitious characters, an 'elsewhere' posturing as here and now, a monotonous 'once upon a time' in which we choose to believe as simply and reasonably as children listening to a fairy tale? The literary phenomenon can't be defined more precisely. If we try to separate it from its phantoms and illusions it simply disintegrates (in this respect literature is as dead today as Nietzsche's god, except that such corpses, as we all know, have long lives and, until further notice, the prophecies concerning them are taking a very long time to come true).

So, for the time being tradition is left out in the dark, and novelty optimistically claims its right to the title—with nothing but the fact of its emergence as warranty. (Twenty years ago the 'nouveau roman' was the first to dare define modernity in this off-hand way without realising that 'modernity' isn't a question of age and that the new grows shabby very quickly if it doesn't take the trouble to get its position clear together with the reasons motivating its use of words and images and its inevitable break with tradition.) When creativity rejects the notions of authority and legitimacy implicitly accepted since Homer, doubts and convictions cease to matter as do such questions as whether literature is a vocation, an art or a profession, and what miracle enables it to presume that its subjective vagaries answer the public's basic requirements. The 'nouveau romancier' who owes nothing to the past would be seen either as uninhibitedly submitting to his imperative need to write, or as the interpreter of the contemporary scene—a role for which his first-hand experience undoubtedly qualifies him, besides relieving him of every responsibility. Forasmuch as it is possible to ascribe definite ends to such a vague school of thought, today's modernity appears to follow two radically opposed trends which, together, contribute to one and the same negation: on the one hand it advocates a 'spontaneous' form of writing, ever-available, self-responsible and self-regulated; on the other it aims at being no more than the mediator of ideas, a revolutionary agent whose specific value is unimportant compared to its potential efficacy. Writing is either an instinctive, emotional outpouring, the word made act, and literature becomes a happening (erotic, sadistic, narcissitic) which provokes elementary sensations and nervous reactions and is modelled as much as possible on everyday life. Or on the other hand writing is at the

service of advanced ideologies, borrowing from
science and technology not only ready-made concepts,
but even their vocabulary. In the first case the writer
is—or purports to be—in a sort of linguistic limbo
where words are not yet fully-fledged. In the second
his 'message' must conform to certain notions of good
and bad rather than truth and falsity, dictated by
extra-literary powers without any literary preoccupations whatsoever. Yet despite the dissimilar motivations of these two types of writing, they achieve
more or less the same end. For in both cases literature
ceases to be a distinct medium of communication and
assumes the urgency of a perishable-goods factory.
But the disintegration of literature into ideological
clichés or instinctual urges is possible only because of
our endemic belief in the magic power of the printed
page.

While modernity hesitates between these two
solutions it could do worse than to hark back to
Kafka's Hunger Artist and the dilemma he solves by
suicide—the artist, reduced by his eccentricity to
refusing all nourishment and letting creation feed on
his own substance, must either recover his appetite or
give up his place to the 'living panther' whose
unquestionable beauty is a tangible refutation of an
over-sophisticated art. For surely this poor Narcissus
feeding his art on the sad remnants of his own flesh, is
already dead, murdered by his own presumptuousness

and the public's indifference to his absurd performance. The panther is there, in possession of the cage
where literature is slowly starving to death in retribution for the unnatural sacrifice it expects from
existence and for its disdain for ordinary nourishment.
It might be objected that the fifty-year-old dilemma
has lost much of its urgency, that things have changed
since Kafka tried to solve it and that if a choice must
still be made there is no reason why it should be
between absolute natural beauty and the Hunger
Artist's doubtful and rarely accepted message. And it's
true that there isn't a final solution to such matters.
Though to date panther and Hunger Artist have never
survived for long in the same cage, and unless a third
alternative can be found—for instance a modern literature liberated from the tyranny of theology or its substi-
tutes, and able to achieve the panther's unequivocal
beauty and truth—modernity has nothing to offer but
the Hunger Artist's anaemic art.

Moreover the disintegration of art that Kafka's
stories predict seems to be taking place—certain
symptoms would even suggest that it is nearing
completion. For who today asks: What is literature?—
which was precisely the Hunger Artist's question.
Rather, with the American student mentioned by
Serge Doubrovsky, we ask: What's it for? Which isn't
really a question but a relentless assertion, something
like a full-stop. In this context to ask what literature is

for is really to answer the question. And indeed what use is literature to someone who can't understand that Oscar Wilde could say in real earnest that the greatest sorrow of his life was the death of Rubempré in *Splendeur et misère des courtisanes*, doesn't consider that the opening sentence of *Bouvard et Pécuchet* is a more significant event than many things which have happened, doesn't get sufficiently involved with fictitious characters to be enthralled by their fictitious loves and hates, and doesn't share Hebbel's mad belief that he can 'Shake the world awake' by virtue of the printed page? What use is it in the end to those who don't feel akin to Don Quixote, the father of Western literature? That clever young man was quite right to ask such a question since literature isn't and never was *for* anything, and that is precisely its unfathomable mystery.

Even if that impertinent (or pertinent) question didn't correspond to a general attitude, it would still be worthy of consideration for its sobering implications (once upon a time it would merely have shocked and the culprit would have been dismissed as illiterate). But literature is no longer convincing. It has lost its glamour and is no more exciting than any of culture's other products. Let it prove the contrary if it is still capable of vindicating its rights, but it can't count on its reputation to do so. It must resign itself to being just one more controllable commodity or realise

once and for all that it is an outdated legend. In other
words it will have to make a final choice between self-
assertion and a sincere self-examination unless it is to
become the last surviving myth in an age that will not
or dare not believe in mythology.

Thus literature is confronted with the fatal question
it has always tried to avoid—except for rare moments
of lucidity when the question was its main topic. Had
it consented to answer earlier would its reign have
been extended? Who can tell? The fact is that it didn't
and that the odd writer who broke the rule of silence
was seldom heard (never being the sort of person to
attract followers but rather an over-demanding, over-
lucid character too much like the Hunger Artist to
serve as a model). Cervantes, that prophetic and
unrelenting critic of romantic writing, deliberately
wove into the texture of his work the indictment of
sanctified literature. But he was sadly misunderstood
even by reactionaries who, much later and on a
different battlefield, championed the cause of disillusionment. For although last century's intellectual
upheavals were serious enough they had surprisingly
little effect on literary sanctity and all the superstitions
it involves. Theoreticians may well have reconstituted
hierarchies, turned everything upside-down and
attempted to establish a genetics of literature, but they
were nonetheless awed by the mystery surrounding
and protecting literature's impenetrable mystery. To

mention only Marx and Freud, who in different ways and at different times made short shrift of traditional concepts, it must be admitted that neither seriously questioned the exaggerated consideration that works of fiction officially enjoy in contemporary culture (officially, not effectively, for owing to a further paradox, such official consideration is usually maintained against a backdrop of total indifference). While demolishing the ideological superstructures upon which literature is primarily based, Marx rekindled the ancient belief that a true writer, whatever his faults, illusions and misconceptions, sees more, and more clearly than the man in the street. In all other respects he may be bigoted and riddled with outdated superstitions, but thanks to his art he possesses a peculiar visionary lucidity and assumes the 'mission' to reveal hitherto unsuspected social contradictions through the interplay of fictitious characters.

As to Freud, although he was the first to provide a consistent theory of the psychic processes involved in creativity, he was always very cautious in his approach to such intellectual activities, as though he were afraid of committing a sacrilege. And if he cast more light than anyone else on the hidden primitive sources from which a writer's vocation flows, he nonetheless preserved all his life the same deep-felt veneration for the *Dichter*—a veneration which, when otherwise directed he did not hesitate to condemn (thus for him the mystic and the philosopher were nothing but pernicious promoters of illusion whom only the undiscerning would idolise). For once the great overturner of idols was remarkably faint-hearted, conforming to taboos religiously observed by the elite of his day and apparently quite unaware of this chink in his armour. For him, as for all those who seek the truth by means of a systematic disillusionment, writing was the one exception to the rule, preserving its sanctity on account of its educative virtues (the *Dichter* knows instinctively what the analyst labours to discover) and especially its unfailing ability to save.

The writer, analysable as a man but untouchable as a creator, his lofty mission thus confirmed, could continue to count on the mystery of his inspiration to justify the social significance of his fictions. And Freud undoubtedly contributed to this cult when he detected the writer's ability to communicate directly with his unconscious psychic activity and presented him as the suffering hero who takes upon himself the sufferings of all mankind while at the same time providing a salutary 'catharsis' for the sick and the deranged. Martyr and scapegoat, healer and provider of perfection into the bargain, Freud's writer had no more cause for complaint than his predecessors. In fact he had less since analytical science, instead of forcing him to see himself for what he was, set him up among the demi-gods of mythology.

True here and there writers have reacted against this heroic image by introducing themselves half-mockingly as clowns, mountebanks, illusionists and charlatans (Jean Starobinsky nicely describes the role of the 'artist as mountebank' whereby the heirs of Romanticism prove their marginality). But such self-portraits are usually more complacent than lucid and merely contribute some variety and novelty to the literary circus.

So it would seem that apart from the occasional Don Quixote whose stories are inspired by the conflict between literary faith and commonsense, nobody is aware of the fact that writers and their works are so grossly overestimated that any book, however undistinguished, always retains some of the authority and glamour of the Holy Scriptures. How can a novelist's personal fictions or a poet's emotional outpourings tell us something momentous about existence or influence it in any way? Why does nobody see the joke when Balzac asserts that he is 'History's secretary' and that he competes with the registry office? How can telling stories enable one to right wrongs or to be a true prophet? Why are novelists generally supposed to know all the mysteries of life and society when they tend to be so exceptionally incapable and unpractical in their own personal affairs? And why, since they are so often lacking in self-control, should they be chosen as spiritual guides and then blamed for their blunders when their alleged far-sightedness happens to lead in the wrong direction? Fictional literature shows very little interest in questions such as whether its means are suited to its ends and whether or not it fulfils its undertakings. Like Don Quixote it probably thinks that 'these are matters which do not have to be thoroughly proved', and that the old theory of the 'magicians' is still the best explanation of its magic. But even here it has to keep quiet, and in the ensuing silence the sacriligious question: What's it for? rings out with increasing distinctness heralding its death.

According to Don Quixote books owe their impact on existence to the spell they cast because they are not made by writers but by black or white magicians who predetermine the nature of this impact. Not much has since been said about the 'mysterious' sources from which literary art acquires its high reputation. Though obviously this doesn't amount to a great deal—it was inadequate in Cervantes' day, and now, when intellectual achievement lays such stress on deflating illusions, the theory of the magicians can't have many adherents. The inextricable wrangle between Don Quixote, the Priest and the Barber had acquired serious proportions (incidentally the Priest and the Barber were already asking 'What's it for?', but although they had the last word they look very small in the light of Don Quixote's madness), because whatever the magicians may say, the time has come when the secrets of their spell-binding activity must be divulged—unless this activity chooses to become obsolete it cannot continue to avoid inspection on the basis of its *a priori* impenetrability. For modern scepticism respects nothing and literature can't go on proclaiming that it is the only surviving blind faith, the only kind of belief that can still hoodwink it. It must choose between thoroughly providing itself or, if it prefers to emulate Don Quixote and declare that it doesn't pertain to the order of verifiable things, becoming one more nostalgic chapter-heading in our archeological files.

*

Insofar as literature now refuses to go on 'telling itself stories' it would seem that it is taking the dilemma seriously at last and has opted for a healthier attitude. However, a rejection of the superstitions on which it once relied doesn't necessarily imply a clearer outlook and a greater reliability. Not telling oneself stories too easily leads to not telling stories at all—in other words to depriving the narrative of its main appeal and, what is more, of the power to evoke which, after all, is its sole purpose (the narrative's aim is to be credible and one of the paradoxes of literary fiction is that the more pains it takes to present its fictions as truth the more credible it becomes). While the Founding Fathers of modernity knew that it required more than sensible resolutions to solve their problems and therefore made up stories involving precisely such problems (the story of Don Quixote is the story of literature and so are the stories of Tristram Shandy, Ulysses and Bouvard and Pécuchet, though in the latter case the story is too good and gripping to be really conclusive, which accounts for its ending in a perpetual recapitulation), today problems have evicted narrative. They are presented unadorned in a sort of intellectual limbo where invention—whether spontaneous or carefully processed—corresponds strictly to some pre-existing theory. The 'nouveau roman' and 'nouvelle critique' agree at least on this point, though their ways have otherwise parted: *telling a story* is a thing of the past since it involves literature in dubious preoccupations with romantic constructions which distract it from its real purpose by literally cramping its style. The novelist is no longer History's secretary, the righter of wrongs and arbitrator of good and evil. Neither is he an expert on an unsavoury brew of World History, love affairs and gossip spiced with a perfunctory pinch of psychology. Moreover his heart was never really in such things. He only tried to believe in the validity of his inventions and will now admit honestly that he hasn't anything particular to say and therefore will simply give free rein to his art in works unadulterated by parasitical thought and emotional pollution (whence the term 'white novel' applied by Bernard Dort to such ideal products). Thus Robbe-Grillet, shocked by the delusions of realism in which Balzac *et alia* indulged, wilfully omits any allusion to what his fictional characters look like, what they think or even who they are. And while unable to avoid altogether the sort of story he detests—indeed those he tells are sufficiently involved to have won him a certain amount of censure—he does his best to make it fragmented and incoherent. True his successors are more consistent since, not content with ridding the narrative of the Quixotic enchanter's superfluous contributions—or disenchanting it at the risk of disenchanting the reader—they go so far as to eliminate anything that might remotely be construed as coherent plot or, to quote Roland Barthes, as 'a fabricated story'. Thus criticism—or the section of literature known as 'discursive' and termed 'secondary' by the Germans to stress the fact that it follows the other both chronologically and hierarchically—is now directly involved with fictional composition, laying down the rules by which it stands or falls (this intrusion of theory into the cage was not foreseen in the prophecy, but is less absurd than it might seem since *nimble* theories aspire more or less in vain to the panther's spontaneity). The result is a considerable reshuffling of traditional genres to enable 'secondary' literature (now promoted to the first rank) to acquire the status of Art without foregoing the advantages of its function. The rules of the game where fictitious beings are supposed to create for the benefit of real beings another world consistent with the one we know, or an alluring elsewhere, these rules are no longer what matters. What is important is the recently discovered linguistic essence, *the verbal essence, neither real nor fictitious, inaccessible to understanding and to the imagination* which, according to Roland Barthes, has no other function than to let itself glide '*along an absent story*', its virtue residing in the fact that it can be neither consumed nor desired. The novel is gauged by its spontaneity *prior to intention and choice* (Philippe Sollers) and not, as superstition would have it, by the '*exaggerated symbol-laden language common to fabricated stories*' (Barthes) which prematurely arrests the elusive flow of reality. Such outmoded language—or *emotional overflow which ejects the author from himself*—is and has always been a camouflaged deceit which must be eradicated in order that the *language of truth* may finally be heard. However, since the only language we possess is so outmoded, redundant and blameworthy, Roland Barthes has every right to assert that we will have to debunk '*not only institutionalised social literature but subjective literature as well.*'

Sartre once said that man is someone who tells himself stories. This is unquestionably true and such incurable mythomania probably accounts for the tremendous success of literature as institutionalised story-telling, as well as for the disrepute in which it is held whenever puritanical reaction sets in. However since Freud's scientific study of dreams we can't ignore the fact that all the stories we invent have a precise meaning and that if such a meaning seems extravagant or even nonexistent to our conscious minds this is because of its intimate relation to our primal mental and emotional experience of repressed parricidal and incestuous desires. First undergone as a perilous inner tragedy which gradually subsides and is consequently forgotten, the Oedipal experience is remarkable in that it is never resolved otherwise than in the imagination, so that it never ceases to be a mental obstacle and stimulus, something the imagination continually seeks to avoid and incessantly expresses. The youthful human Oedipus, still too frail to cope with the violence of impulses which arrest his development, tries, since he is nonetheless obliged to develop, to evade the constriction of conflict in a supreme effort of the imagination to translate these basic elements of experience into 'fictions' which will give him at least the illusion of controlling his own fate. And the inventive youngster, forced to resolve the major crisis life's intractability represents, is not less successful than the adult novelist who, in fact, does no more than imitate him. He is already wholly involved in literature for better or for worse, indeed he is a living proof of literature's right to assert, despite its inherent duplicity, that it is only telling the truth and that by turning subjective mythomania into a common asset it remains an off-shoot of mythology after all.

Thus the theoretician is entitled to be equally dismissive of the stories we tell ourselves, those we tell others and of that last stronghold of mythology, institutionalised literature. For all stories derive from the same source, and if the source is corrupt then they are all equally blameworthy. Literature is reflected in every story it tells. It merges institution with the art of story-telling and continues to tell stories because story-telling has become an institution. We must either take it as it comes with its tendentious stories and its overrated History, or make up our minds to do away with it. Apparently its worst enemies have already made the choice—since it can't be 'purified' it must be destroyed.

But isn't the notion of a 'pure' narrator who, as subject, hero and sole beneficiary of the story has no other aim than to avoid the Oedipal tale which might emerge, just one more story we are telling ourselves? For after all a narrator merging into his own words, a theoretician of ever-evaded history, is really nothing but a 'pure' narcissistic puppet precariously established beyond communicability and wholly absorbed in self-contemplation. Dream for dream, what's the point of such a change? The much blamed and blameworthy literature of the past had to its credit at least the fact that it believed it was capable of bridging the gap between its own dreams and those of all mankind. And at its best it could communicate such a belief—indeed therein lay its wisdom and its folly. Whereas the disillusioned narratives of today are content to bewitch themselves without ever letting the reader penetrate the mystery of their magic. And it must be admitted that it requires some courage to give up trying to please and to court disfavour with such dogged determination.—In so doing can the new dream hope to avoid the fate of those outdated seductive illusions whose demise it observes with such detachment? That is hardly likely. But whatever its fate, it will certainly not be accused of over-staying its welcome—nor of being over-seductive.

*

Obviously the self-indulgence of the *absent story* school is far removed from the anguish, shame and despair of a Chekhov when he felt he might have been guilty of trying to dazzle the reader without giving him anything of positive value. Talent seemed highly suspect to the Russian. It degraded those who possessed it and was detrimental to the reader if it conveyed nothing beyond itself. Moreover: 'In the

present state of affairs a writer's existence is meaningless and the greater his talent the more strange and
incomprehensible is his role . . . '. Thus on the one
hand it is a pleasurable duty to dispatch a dying art,
while on the other anguish and doubt turn the
obstacles in the writer's way into imperatives to carry
on. For Chekhov goes on writing with the obstinate
courage of despair, goes on shattering his illusions by
adding his share to the general meaninglessness.
perhaps out of consideration for meaninglessness or,
more likely, out of humility.

*

Whichever may seem to be the best way of dispatching
literature—the straightforward death-sentence or
hacking it down to the roots in the hope that it will re-
sprout more satisfactorily—at the moment it is just
like one of those empty, gaping buildings which might
be either already crumbling or in the process of
construction. It bears the stigma of temporality with
all its ambiguity and distress.

*

I must jot down this observation made by André
Breton on the subject discussed above: 'Luckily the
days of psychological fiction with romantic plots are

recounted [*sic*] . . . '. The slip is so apposite that I can't bring myself to correct it: was the account charged to the poor dying creature only one more story re-counted? Indeed after fifty years the dying creature is not yet dead.

*

If Nietzsche was right in believing that grammar is the only god we still want to and must worship after all the others have failed, how many of us are justified today in claiming to be atheists!

*

According to Sophroniska, the psychoanalyst who treats little Boris in Gide's *les Faux-monnayeurs*: 'All that is created by the intellect alone is false . . . '. But what has she and what has Gide to say of that which is created without any intelligence at all?

*

Of sweeping judgements.—A revolutionary thinker, that is, one sufficiently strong and independent to take a solitary stand against established opinion without fearing the consequences, tends to be judged indiscriminately as a total innovator. Whether he is an artist, a writer or a philosopher he will be summarily classified as a whole, equally mature and evolved in every respect and entirely intent on total revolution. Anyone who disturbs our general somnolence by forcing us to perceive what over-familiarity conceals must be revolutionary in every walk of life and the new he creates has to be beautiful into the bargain and completely flawless. Whence his disciples' bitter disappointment—though idolisation of this kind can obviously only lead to disappointment—when they realise that their revolutionary genius is in many ways inexplicably and shamefully regressive where their expectations of a final break-through to total solutions was concerned. Once it becomes clear that he is for instance a woman-hater, politically reactionary or ethically conservative he is considered inconsistent and generally despised without a thought for his motives or any attempt at discriminating between a substantial intellectual failing and a simple opinion which, all things considered, can be neither right nor wrong but merely favourably or unfavourably received by a given society at a given time. Paradoxically a misguided opinion tends to cast a greater slur on the thinker's reputation than do his seemingly more seriously compromising blunders and faulty arguments. (Thus Freud, whose opinions don't always conform to what we consider *today* to be the only opinions an enlightened mind could *ever* have upheld, is frequently and anachronistically condemned. Conversely Hegel remains, as far as I know, unscathed,—though if we think of some of the atrocities he calmly professes—for instance his views on negroes—we can't help being struck, not so much by his lack of enlightenment, as by a disturbing propensity to talk nonsense.)

*

In Simone de Beauvoir's *Les Mandarins* the character who purports to be a psychoanalyst declares without turning a hair: 'They found I had a rather pronounced Oedipus complex . . . '! I know that novelists—not without reason—feel they don't have to be thoroughly informed on all the topics they discuss since their ignorance is never held against them. But all the same the author might have obtained a minimum of information, were it only to enable the reader to believe in the character's profession!

*

But generally speaking the novel's relation to psychology is rather vague. Insofar as the novelist is the undisputed expert on love affairs and all things concerning them directly or indirectly, he can only look down on the professional psychologist who, luckily, is too well aware of his own shortcomings to dissuade him. Since the novelist has been granted the ability to penetrate the human psyche and to reproduce what he finds there in every detail, he isn't really interested in acquiring further knowledge on the subject. Or, should such matters attract his fancy, it is never with the object of giving his characters and their problems more depth and complexity, but merely to add to his cast the odd psychologist or psychiatrist whose bigotry and inefficiency usually serve to show up the hero's intellectual abilities (no one has such a raw deal as the psychoanalyst, nor is anyone quite so redundant—from Krokovsky in *The Magic Mountain* to Sophroniska in *Les Faux-monnayeurs* passing through a number of less famous examples I can't find a single one who isn't made up out of approximation and cliché). Apparently the simple fact of holding the psychoanalyst up to ridicule exempts the novelist from applying to his own characters the insights he might glean from him. As if instead of describing a falling object we brought a physicist into the room to explain the law of gravity and forthwith antagonise all those who question the validity of this law or find it distasteful.

*

Arthur Adamov was in the habit of encouraging himself to carry on writing a text with which he was only partially satisfied by exclaiming out loud: 'It's worth what it's worth!' One day to our great amusement he exclaimed by mistake: 'It's worth what I want!' Though in fact this was a remarkable case of the baffler baffled by his own truth, his slip of the tongue was revelatory, for it proved that for him more than for any other writer the narcissistic 'what I want' was never seriously troubled by the 'what it's worth' of public opinion.

*

Nothing is more essential to intellectual hygiene than a regular mythoscopic examination. True it requires an analytic apparatus of exceptional precision and a practically unlimited store of patience.

*

Lautréamont was right—nothing will ever erase an intellectual stain. But how can the stain be detected when the fabric is one vast blemish?

*

After which there is no last word.—The death-dance that literature executes in the hope of finding oblivion and extinction is like Strindberg's in that it is endless. The only sort of conclusion it can find is the exhausted Captain's: 'Let's keep going!' which ensures his unending torture.—So be it: let's keep going . . . .